Biography Today

Profiles of People of Interest to Young Readers

Volume 19
Issue 1
January 2010

Cherie D. Abbey
Managing Editor

Omnigraphics

*P.O. Box 31-1640
Detroit, MI 48231-1640*

Cherie D. Abbey, *Managing Editor*

Peggy Daniels, Joan Goldsworthy, Laurie Lanzen Harris, Kevin Hillstrom, Laurie Hillstrom, and Diane Telgen, *Sketch Writers*

Allison A. Beckett and Mary Butler, *Research Staff*

* * *

Peter E. Ruffner, *Publisher*
Matthew P. Barbour, *Senior Vice President*

* * *

Elizabeth Collins, *Research and Permissions Coordinator*
Kevin M. Hayes, *Operations Manager*
Cherry Stockdale, *Permissions Assistant*

Shirley Amore, Martha Johns, and Kirk Kauffmann, *Administrative Staff*

Special thanks to Frederick G. Ruffner for creating this series.

ISSN 1058-2347 • ISBN 978-0-7808-1058-7

Library of Congress Cataloging-in-Publication Data

This book is printed on acid-free paper meeting the ANSI Z39.48 Standard. The infinity symbol that appears above indicates that the paper in this book meets that standard.

Printed in the United States

Contents

Preface

Biography Today is a magazine designed and written for the young reader—ages 9 and above—and covers individuals that librarians and teachers tell us that young people want to know about most: entertainers, athletes, writers, illustrators, cartoonists, and political leaders.

The Plan of the Work

The publication was especially created to appeal to young readers in a format they can enjoy reading and readily understand. Each issue contains approximately 10 sketches arranged alphabetically. Each entry provides at least one picture of the individual profiled, and bold-faced rubrics lead the reader to information on birth, youth, early memories, education, first jobs, marriage and family, career highlights, memorable experiences, hobbies, and honors and awards. Each of the entries ends with a list of easily accessible sources designed to lead the student to further reading on the individual and a current address. Retrospective entries are also included, written to provide a perspective on the individual's entire career.

Biographies are prepared by Omnigraphics editors after extensive research, utilizing the most current materials available. Those sources that are generally available to students appear in the list of further reading at the end of the sketch.

Indexes

Cumulative indexes are an important component of *Biography Today*. Each issue of the *Biography Today* General Series includes a Cumulative Names Index, which comprises all individuals profiled in *Biography Today* since the series began in 1992. In addition, we compile three other indexes: the Cumulative General Index, Places of Birth Index, and Birthday Index. See our web site, www.biographytoday.com, for these three indexes, along with the Names Index. All *Biography Today* indexes are cumulative, including all individuals profiled in both the General Series and the Subject Series.

Our Advisors

This series was reviewed by an Advisory Board comprising librarians, children's literature specialists, and reading instructors to ensure that the concept of this publication—to provide a readable and accessible biographical magazine for young readers—was on target. They evaluated the title as it developed, and their suggestions have proved invaluable. Any errors, however, are ours alone. We'd like to list the Advisory Board members, and to thank them for their efforts.

Gail Beaver
Adjunct Lecturer
University of Michigan
Ann Arbor, MI

Cindy Cares
Youth Services Librarian
Southfield Public Library
Southfield, MI

Carol A. Doll
School of Information Science and Policy
University of Albany, SUNY
Albany, NY

Kathleen Hayes-Parvin
Language Arts Teacher
Birney Middle School
Southfield, MI

Karen Imarisio
Assistant Head of Adult Services
Bloomfield Twp. Public Library
Bloomfield Hills, MI

Rosemary Orlando
Director
St. Clair Shores Public Library
St. Clair Shores, MI

Our Advisory Board stressed to us that we should not shy away from controversial or unconventional people in our profiles, and we have tried to follow their advice. The Advisory Board also mentioned that the sketches might be useful in reluctant reader and adult literacy programs, and we would value any comments librarians might have about the suitability of our magazine for those purposes.

Your Comments Are Welcome

Our goal is to be accurate and up-to-date, to give young readers information they can learn from and enjoy. Now we want to know what you think. Take a look at this issue of *Biography Today,* on approval. Write or call me with your comments. We want to provide an excellent source of biographical information for young people. Let us know how you think we're doing.

Cherie Abbey
Managing Editor, *Biography Today*
Omnigraphics, Inc.
P.O. Box 31-1640
Detroit, MI 48231-1640
www.omnigraphics.com

Congratulations!

Congratulations to the following individuals and libraries who are receiving a free copy of *Biography Today*, Vol. 19, No. 1, for suggesting people who appear in this issue.

Adrian Alvarez, San Saba, TX

Paul Bishette, Silas Bronson Library, Waterbury, CT

Michael Bosquez, San Saba, TX

Judi Chelekis, Vassar High School Library, Vassar, MI

Ashley Daly, Ardmore High School, Ardmore, AL

Rachel Q. Davis, Thomas Memorial Library, Cape Elizabeth, ME

Lori Drummond, Washington Middle School, Aurora, IL

Regina Floyd, Chicago, IL

Kathleen Gorman, Cardinal Joseph Bernardin Catholic School, Orland Hills, IL

Cierra Huggins, Toledo, OH

Tyisha James, Tampa, FL

Richard Kimball, Sherman, ME

Amy Lucio, Cedar Creek Intermediate, Cedar Creek, TX

Steven Ott Jr., Covington School, Oak Lawn, IL

Melina Rangel, Bell Gardens, CA

Jessica Sanchez, Dr. William R. Peck Middle School, Holyoke, MA

Lisa Scharf, Memorial Junior High, Mentor, OH

Jim Steinke, Cottage Grove High School, Cottage Grove, WI

Loretta Talbert, North County Regional Library, Huntersville, NC

Josh Wallace, Joliet Public Library, Joliet, IL

Beyoncé 1981-

American Singer, Songwriter, Producer, and Actress
Grammy-Winning Creator of *I Am … Sasha Fierce*
and Star of *Dreamgirls*

[An entry on the group Destiny's Child, with significant coverage of Beyoncé, appeared in Biography Today, *April 2001, and the* Biography Today *2001 Annual Cumulation.]*

BIRTH

Beyoncé Giselle Knowles was born on September 4, 1981, in Houston, Texas. She was the first child of Mathew Knowles, a medical equipment salesman, and his wife Tina, a hairdresser and salon owner. Her unusual first name, which rhymes with "fiancé," was taken from Beyincé, which was Tina Knowles's maiden name. Beyoncé has a younger sister, Solange, who also became a professional performer and songwriter.

Beyoncé started out her professional career with the group Destiny's Child, and at that point she used her full name, Beyoncé Knowles. Later, after she became a solo performer, she began using just her first name, Beyoncé.

YOUTH

Beyoncé's parents had loved music in their own youth, and their daughters grew up with music in the house. "My parents used to sing to me all the time," the singer remembered. "My dad tells me that as a baby, I would go crazy whenever I heard music, and I tried to dance before I could even walk." Since Beyoncé was a shy child, her parents hoped to bring her out of her shell by giving her dance lessons. Her teacher discovered her singing talent and encouraged her to perform in a school talent show. She won the competition by singing John Lennon's "Imagine," astonishing her parents with her powerful voice. This led to singing lessons and many more victories in talent shows. By 1990, Beyoncé had joined Girl's Tyme, a local girl group managed by Andretta Tillman. Although the lineup changed as girls dropped in and out, Beyoncé became a mainstay of Girl's Tyme, which performed at events around the Houston area.

When Tillman became ill, Mathew Knowles helped manage Girl's Tyme, which by now included Kelly Rowland. Because Rowland's mother worked as a nanny and often lived away from home, Kelly came to live with Beyoncé's family. The Knowleses gave the girls every opportunity to polish their skills. Mathew Knowles made them sing while jogging, so they could develop the stamina to sing and dance at the same time. He built a deck in their back yard, providing a place to practice routines. Tina Knowles had the girls perform for customers in her hair salon, and their feedback helped the girls develop their stage presence. Summer vacations were full of dance rehearsals, voice lessons, and interview training, which Beyoncé considered fun. "It was my time to create dance routines and vocal arrangements. It seemed like playtime," she recalled. Girl's Tyme was excited when they made the finals of the nationally syndicated television talent show "Star Search" in 1992. When they lost to an adult rock band the group was crushed, thinking their dream of a music career was over. "We almost went crazy from crying," Beyoncé noted. "A lot was riding on that performance."

Mathew Knowles had faith in his daughter's talent. After the loss on "Star Search," he left his high-paying job at Xerox to take over management of the group. By this time it had settled on four members—Beyoncé, Rowland, LeToya Luckett, and LaTavia Roberson—and had gone through several name changes before settling on Destiny's Child. Mathew Knowles took the group to California for record company auditions. In 1993 they signed with Elektra Records and moved to Atlanta to work on a first recording. Unfortunately, the record company dropped them in 1995 before they could produce an album. The girls returned home, seemingly to start all over again. The efforts put a strain on the Knowles family, and Beyoncé's parents separated briefly when she was 14. By 1996, however, the family was reunited and Destiny's Child had a new contract, this time with Columbia Records.

"My parents used to sing to me all the time," Beyoncé remembered. "My dad tells me that as a baby, I would go crazy whenever I heard music, and I tried to dance before I could even walk."

”

EDUCATION

Beyoncé attended private elementary schools as a child, earning mostly As and Bs. She briefly attended Houston's High School for Visual and Performing Arts and the Alief Elsik High School. Because she was a working performer by the time she was in ninth grade, she was privately tutored for the rest of her teens. She earned the equivalent of a high school diploma in 2000.

CAREER HIGHLIGHTS

Destiny's Child

It took a while for Destiny's Child to create their first album, as the record company sought appropriate material for a young girl group to record. They paired the group with superstar producers like Wyclef Jean and Jermaine Dupri, who helped the group record tracks over the next two years. In the meantime the group contributed the single "Killing Time" to the *Men in Black* soundtrack in 1997 and got to meet the film's co-star, rapper-actor Will Smith. Tina Knowles took over as the group's stylist during this time, using her sewing experience, fashion sense, and knowledge of the girls' personalities to craft an image they felt comfortable with. They released their first single in 1997, and "No, No, No" hit No. 1 on the R&B (rhythm & blues) chart and No. 3 on the *Billboard* Hot 100 list. When they

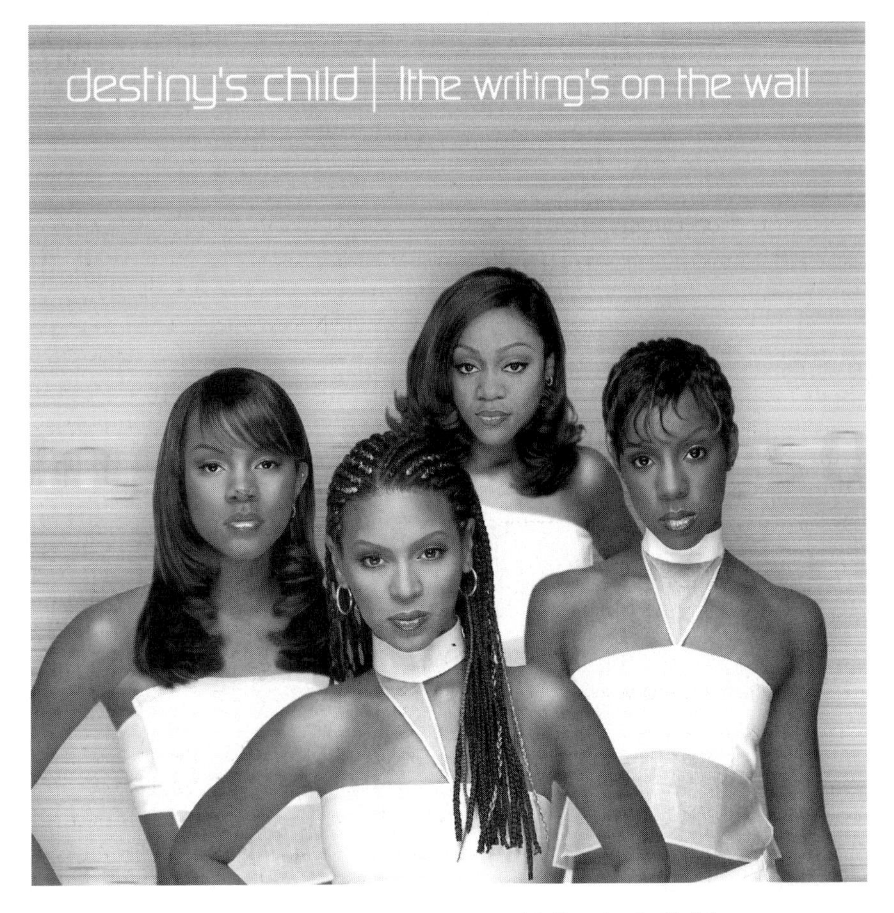

Beyoncé's first big success came with Destiny's Child.

released the self-titled album *Destiny's Child* in 1998, it hit No. 15 on the R&B album charts and was certified gold.

The group quickly followed up their first album with a second, *The Writing's on the Wall,* in 1999. This time Beyoncé co-wrote 10 of the tracks, rather than just a couple, including the first single, "Bills, Bills, Bills." The song, featuring Beyoncé and Rowland telling a deadbeat boyfriend to leave, became the group's first No. 1 single. A second single, "Bug a Boo," only reached No. 33, but it helped establish the group's style: fast singing (usually featuring Beyoncé) that sometimes approached rapping, and themes of strength, independence, and girl power. Controversy struck before the group released their next single, when Luckett and Roberson asked for a new manager. They accused Mathew Knowles of favoring Beyoncé and Rowland. In response, he kicked the girls out of the group and found replacements. He brought in Michelle Williams and Farrah Franklin to fill in for public appearances. Eventually Franklin left too, claiming control issues were the reason for her departure.

But the controversy didn't slow the group down. Even as Luckett and Roberson sued the group and their manager, Destiny's Child continued as a trio made up of Beyoncé, Kelly Rowland, and Michelle Williams. Their next single produced the monster hit "Say My Name," which spent 11 weeks in the Top 10, including three weeks at No. 1. It boosted *The Writing's on the Wall* to No. 5 on the album chart, selling more than 10 million copies worldwide. A fourth single, "Jumpin', Jumpin'" landed in the Top 20 for radio airplay. In 2000 the group also earned their first Grammy Awards, with "Say My Name" earning statues for Best R&B Song and Best R&B Vocal Performance by a Duo or Group. Beyoncé was philosophical about all the turmoil: "I think in order for your group to be successful your story has to be interesting. Our story was very squeaky clean, so I thank God for the controversy. I'm happy because it helps me sell records." Later, however, she admitted to a period of depression following the departure of her childhood friends from the group. During this time, she sought solace in church services and worked out her emotions by writing songs.

Those songs appeared on the trio's next album, the 2001 smash *Survivor.* Not only did Beyoncé co-write all but one track on the album, she co-produced most of the tracks as well. The first single, "Independent Women, Part 1," debuted as part of the *Charlie's Angels* film soundtrack and sat at No. 1 for 10 weeks. The second single, "Survivor," charted at No. 2, but also inspired a defamation lawsuit from Luckett and Roberson, who claimed the line "You thought I wouldn't sell without ya/ sold 9 million" violated the terms of their agreement in settling their previous lawsuit. That suit was also settled out of court, and Destiny's Child continued to rule the charts: the single "Bootylicious" spent two weeks at No. 1, "Emotion" hit No. 10, and the album *Survivor* debuted at No. 1 and sold over 3.7 million copies in 2001. It earned the group a slew of awards, including a Grammy for Best R&B Vocal Performance by a Duo or Group ("Survivor"), an MTV Video Music Award for Best R&B Video ("Survivor"), American Music Awards for Favorite Soul/R&B Group and Favorite Pop/Rock Album, and a Teen Choice Award for Choice Pop Group.

Going Solo

Destiny's Child was one of the hottest groups of the early 2000s, but there was also speculation that Beyoncé, as the group's lead singer and song-

Scenes from Beyoncé's early career: performing with Destiny's Child (top); appearing with Mike Myers in Austin Powers in Goldmember; *and releasing her first solo album,* Dangerously in Love.

writer, was looking toward a solo career. It was Beyoncé, not the group, who won the ASCAP Songwriter of the Year Award in 2002—only the second woman, and the first African-American one, to capture that prize. After the singer commented she needed a break from four years of constant rehearsing and touring, rumors spread that Destiny's Child was breaking up. The rumors increased as members took a break to pursue their individual interests. In 2002, Rowland released a solo R&B album and Williams had the best-selling gospel album of that year. Beyoncé, however, decided to focus on developing her acting career.

“

Over the years, Beyoncé has developed a separate persona for her stage shows. "I have someone else that takes over when it's time for me to work and when I'm on stage, this alter ego that I've created that kind of protects me and who I really am."

”

The singer had her first acting experience in the 2001 made-for-MTV musical, "Carmen: A Hip-Hopera." It set the story of Bizet's classic opera *Carmen* in modern times, with Beyoncé in the title role of an aspiring actress whose seduction of a policeman leads to ruin. A *Variety* reviewer noted that "Knowles makes a fine acting debut, and once again makes it clear that she's got a surplus of star power." Although the film was more like an extended music video, it brought her to the attention of Hollywood. For her next film, she earned her first feature film role working with Mike Myers in *Austin Powers in Goldmember* (2002). She played Foxxy Cleopatra, a sexy agent who recalled the heroines of the 1970s black-centered action films. While *Goldmember* didn't get great reviews, several critics noted Beyoncé demonstrated good screen presence in the role. The film earned over $200 million in the U.S. and earned her nominations for Teen Choice, Kids' Choice, and MTV Movie Awards.

In 2003 Beyoncé released her own solo singing project. The album showcased a different, more vulnerable side. "I always held back in Destiny's Child, because I was comfortable in a group," she explained. "I would not lose myself or go all the way." *Dangerously in Love* debuted at No. 1 on the *Billboard* album charts, with help from its first single, "Crazy in Love." This collaboration with rapper (and rumored boyfriend) Jay-Z was the hit of summer 2003, spending eight weeks at No. 1. The next single, "Baby Boy," topped the charts for nine weeks, and the album also produced the Top 10 hits "Naughty Girl" and "Me, Myself, and I." The album earned acclaim from her peers as well, garnering three MTV Music Video Awards and five Grammy Awards, tying a record for a female artist in a single Grammys. *Dangerously in Love* earned Best R&B Album; "Crazy in Love" won Best Rap/Sung Collaboration and Best R&B Song (a songwriting award); "Dangerously in Love 2" brought a trophy for Best Female R&B Vocal Performance; and Beyoncé's duet with Luther Vandross, a remake of "The Closer I Get to You," won Best R&B Performance by a Duo or Group with Vocals.

Not long after her solo release, Beyoncé appeared in her first lead film role, opposite Oscar-winner Cuba Gooding, Jr. in *The Fighting Temptations* (2003). She played Lilly, a single mom who has been kicked out of her church for having a child out of wedlock and who then teams up with Darrin (played by Gooding) to win a choir competition. "I saw a lot of comedic and dramatic opportunities in playing this character, and I knew I'd have a lot of fun with it," she remarked. Although the film didn't perform well at the box office, Beyoncé earned nominations for best actress from the NAACP Image Awards and Black Reel Film Awards. She also co-wrote songs for the film, including "He Still Loves Me," which earned her a Black Reel Film Award for Best Song.

Saying Goodbye to Destiny's Child

By 2004, Beyoncé was a full-fledged superstar, singing the national anthem at the Super Bowl and earning endorsement deals with many major companies. People were surprised when Destiny's Child announced they would release a new album that year, but it made sense to Beyoncé. While seeing how they could grow as solo artists was important, she said, "it's really beautiful to do that and then also have the opportunity to come back together and have the fun we have when we are together. When you have that sort of friendship, recording doesn't feel like work." Their 2004 release *Destiny Fulfilled* was the group's last original album. It debuted at No. 2 on the album charts and topped the R&B album charts. It generated two No. 3 hits, "Lose My Breath" and "Soldier," as well as the Top 25 singles "Girl" and "Cater 2 U." The group—which according to some measurements was the best-selling female group of all time—went on a final tour in 2005 and announced midway they would disband for good after it was over. Nevertheless, they had one last number one album, the 2005 greatest hits collection *#1's.*

Beyoncé had plenty to keep her occupied once Destiny's Child broke up in 2005. Besides her growing acting and solo singing careers, she founded the fashion company House of Deréon with her mother, Tina, who had long been her daughter's costume designer and stylist. The company name—and its designs—were inspired by Beyoncé's grandmother and Tina's

Beyoncé performing with Jay-Z, her future husband, at the 2003 MTV Video Music Awards.

mother, Agnéz Dereon, who had worked as a seamstress. House of Deréon created higher-end gowns, women's wear, and accessories and was sold in boutiques and prestige department stores like Neiman Marcus and Bloomingdale's. Later they created another line with Beyoncé's sister Solange, called Deréon. This line focused on lower-priced sportswear for juniors, to be sold in department stores like Dillard's and Macy's.

"Beyoncé is rarely the focus of tabloid stories, is never caught behaving badly by paparazzi, and declines to speak about her private life. "I've worked too hard and sacrificed too much to do something silly that would mess up the brand I've created all of these years," she noted. "The older I get, the more I think about the amount of influence I have on these young girls, and it's scary sometimes. But I also understand how lucky I am to have that.""

In 2006, on her 25th birthday, Beyoncé released her second solo album, *B'Day*. It debuted at No. 1 on the album chart on the way to selling more than three million copies. Its first single, "Déjà Vu," reached No. 4 and "Ring the Alarm" hit No. 11. But "Irreplaceable" was the monster hit from the album, staying at No. 1 for 10 weeks. *B'Day* won a Grammy for Best Contemporary R&B Album. In spring 2007 Beyoncé released an expanded deluxe edition of the album with several new tracks, some in Spanish. One was a duet with Colombian singing star Shakira, "Beautiful Liar," which became the fastest moving single in *Billboard* history, going from No. 94 to No. 3 in a single week. The song also earned an MTV Video Music Award. Beyoncé supported the album with a lavish worldwide tour called "The Beyoncé Experience," which featured an all-female backing band and dancers, video screens, multiple costume changes, and complex choreography. It played to enthusiastic audiences all over the world, and in 2007 Beyoncé was voted Best International Artist at the American Music Awards, the first African American to earn that honor.

A *Dream* Acting Role

Even as she dominated the music charts, Beyoncé was working on developing her acting career. In 2006 she appeared in *The Pink Panther* with

Beyoncé with Jennifer Hudson in Dreamgirls.

comedy superstar Steve Martin. The film was inspired by the classic 1963 comedy of the same title, about a bumbling French detective (played by Peter Sellers in the original) who manages to solve mysteries in spite of his clumsiness. In this prequel, Beyoncé plays Xenia, a pop star who becomes a suspect when her soccer coach-boyfriend is murdered at the same time his diamond ring is stolen. The actress found filming both fun and challenging. "Many of my scenes were with Steve [Martin], and it was really difficult to stay in character because he is so funny and I never knew what he was going to do," she said. While the film received tepid reviews, it opened at No. 1 and made a respectable $82 million in U.S. box office. Beyoncé recorded a new version of her song "Check on It" for the film—it was originally released with the Destiny's Child collection *#1's*—and it shot to the top of the pop charts and stayed at No. 1 for five weeks.

Later that year the budding actress appeared in the role of a lifetime: a starring turn in *Dreamgirls,* a film based on the Tony Award-winning stage musical from 1982. The story is loosely based on the journey of the Supremes, a Motown girl group of the 1960s whose lead singer, Diana Ross, later became a superstar solo artist. Beyoncé had studied the Supremes' moves as a young singer, and she was thrilled to be cast in the role of Deena Jones, a backup singer in the "Dreamettes" who is promoted to lead singer because of her stunning looks and pop-style voice. This angers former lead singer Effie (played by Oscar-winner Jennifer Hudson), leading the group to break up and Deena to rise to solo stardom under the control of her manager-husband (played by Jamie Foxx). Beyoncé dropped 20 pounds to play the role, which required her to portray both inexperience and independence. She was successful, as a *Daily Variety* critic observed: "Knowles is poised, quietly determined, and beautiful beyond belief, blossoming from innocent teenager to self-possessed star."

Dreamgirls was a both a popular and critical success, earning over $100 million at the box office and landing on many critics' lists of top films of the year. Beyoncé earned several nominations for acting awards, most notably the Golden Globe for best actress in a musical or comedy, but also the NAACP Image, MTV Movie, Satellite, and Black Reel Awards. A new song she co-wrote for the film, "Listen," won a Critics Choice Award for best song from the Broadcast Film Critics Association and was also nominated for a Golden Globe.

Beyoncé worked even harder for her next role, in *Cadillac Records* (2008), which tells the true story of the pioneering record label that introduced artists like Chuck Berry and Bo Diddley to mainstream America. This time she was playing a real person, legendary blues singer Etta James, who broke barriers in the music business but also struggled with heroin addiction. The actress—who also helped produce the film and wrote four songs for the soundtrack—gained 15 pounds for the role and researched drug addiction by visiting rehab centers. (She later donated her entire $4 million salary for the film to Phoenix House, a nationwide group of rehab centers.) The film earned her the best notices of her career, with critics using words like "surprise," "soulful," "bitter and beautifully vulnerable," "inspired and persuasive," and "revelatory" to describe her performance. Beyoncé admitted that she had been particularly inspired by playing James: "She was bold and she did not try to change who she was for anyone," she wrote on her website. Playing her on screen "gave me the strength and the confidence to step out of my comfort zone even more." As she later added in an interview, "That is why I love doing movies so much, because it's not just an art form. It changes my life and my music and the way I look at things."

Expanding Her Horizons

The singer brought that sense of change and exploration to her next recording project, the 2008 double album *I Am ... Sasha Fierce.* The first CD, *I Am...,* was filled with self-reflective ballads like the top five singles "If I Were a Boy" and "Halo." The second disc featured up-tempo numbers, like the smash No.1 hit "Single Ladies (Put a Ring on It)," that represent the booty-shaking performer nicknamed "Sasha Fierce." "I have someone else that takes over when it's time for me to work and when I'm on stage, this alter ego that I've created that kind of protects me and who I really am," Beyoncé explained. *I Am ... Sasha Fierce* debuted at No. 1 on the album chart, selling over four million copies worldwide in its first year. The supporting tour was a top earner of summer 2009, and the video for "Single Ladies" became an internet sensation that was copied throughout pop culture. Inspired by a dance routine by Broadway choreographer Bob Fosse, the video earned the MTV Video of the Year Award and was parodied on television shows like "Saturday Night Live" and "Glee."

> *"Her "Sasha Fierce" image may be sexy and sassy, but Beyoncé considers herself a simple, spiritual woman: "It's a way of life for me. What's more important to me [over image] is the way I treat people, what I think, what I give to other people. When I go back to Houston and go to church and see those people, I feel like the same country girl."*
> "

In 2009, Beyoncé also made her first movie appearance in a role that didn't involve music. In *Obsessed,* she played a wife whose marriage is threatened by a woman stalking her husband. The singer also helped produce the film and was excited about the challenge: "It's the first time I didn't have that [musical] crutch, but after *Cadillac Records,* I had a confidence that I never had before." Although the film was critically panned, it opened at No. 1 and earned over $68 million in U.S. box office. That year also saw the singer-actress featured at the Academy Awards, performing a musical number with host Hugh Jackman. Her most memorable moment of the year, however, was her performance at one of the inaugural balls for President Barack Obama. For many observers, her emotional version of the Etta James's standard "At Last," sung as the first African-American president and first lady danced together, helped symbolize this historic moment.

Beyoncé's most recent release, I Am ... Sasha Fierce, *showcased two sides of her performing persona.*

Despite the potential pitfalls of attaining fame at a young age, Beyoncé has maintained a reputation as a class act, something she first determined to do when she was at a *Men in Black* signing with Will Smith. "He was so nice to every person," she remembered. "I watched him. I knew he had to be tired, and I couldn't believe how nice he was." At the time, she told herself, "I don't care if I ever get that famous, I will always be like him." One example occurred at the 2009 MTV Video Music Awards. When Taylor Swift won Best Female Video Award, she was rudely interrupted during her acceptance speech by rapper Kanye West, who stormed the stage and insisted that Beyoncé should have won. Then, when Beyoncé won the Video of the Year Award, she offered the microphone to Swift. Beyoncé is rarely the focus of tabloid stories, is never caught behaving badly by paparazzi, and declines to speak about her private life. "I've worked too hard and sacrificed too much to do something silly that would mess up the brand I've created all of these years," she noted. "The older I get, the more I think about the amount of influence I have on these young girls, and it's scary sometimes. But I also understand how lucky I am to have that."

Although her life is filled with glamour and excitement, Beyoncé stresses that family is the most important thing to her. Without it, she said, she would be nowhere, because "nobody in the world had confidence and believed in us like my mom and dad." Her father is still her manager as the head of the Urban/Gospel division of Music World Entertainment, the management company that he founded and later sold for $10 million. Her mother is still her stylist and design partner in House of Deréon; her cousin is her personal assistant and frequent songwriting partner; and she has taken her sister Solange on tour as a backup dancer or opening act. Her "Sasha Fierce" image may be sexy and sassy, but Beyoncé considers herself a simple, spiritual woman: "It's a way of life for me. What's more important to me [over image] is the way I treat people, what I think, what I give to other people. When I go back to Houston and go to church and see those people, I feel like the same country girl."

MARRIAGE AND FAMILY

Beyoncé married rapper and music mogul Shawn Corey Carter, known professionally as Jay-Z, on April 4, 2008. The two first worked together on Jay-Z's 2003 hit "Bonnie and Clyde" and dated for several years before their marriage. While they appeared in public at various events, they never spoke of their relationship to the press, and it was several months before they publicly confirmed the wedding took place. The couple has an apartment in Manhattan, as well as a mansion in Scarsdale, New York.

HOBBIES AND OTHER INTERESTS

As a superstar in multiple fields, Beyoncé has little time for hobbies. She enjoys relaxing at home and likes to watch movies or makeover shows. She enjoys fashion, collecting clothes and old costumes, which she may later sell for charity. She devotes time and money to many charitable causes, including public school music programs, children's charities, hunger and disaster relief, cancer and AIDS charities, and church programs. After Hurricane Katrina forced many New Orleans families to relocate to her hometown of Houston, the Knowles family and Kelly Rowland set up the Survivor Foundation, which founded "Destiny Village" to provide cost-free

Beyoncé in an appearance on the "Today" show.

housing for 100 families. The singer also uses her tours to inspire others to help; the final Destiny's Child tour contributed 25 cents of every ticket to Ronald McDonald House Charities, while she partnered with General Mills during her "Beyoncé Experience" tour to include a food drive with each concert.

RECORDINGS

With Destiny's Child

Destiny's Child, 1998
The Writing's on the Wall, 1999
Survivor, 2001
8 Days of Christmas, 2001
This Is the Remix, 2002
Destiny Fulfilled, 2004
#1s, 2005

As Beyoncé

Dangerously in Love, 2003
Live at Wembley, 2004
B'day, 2006, deluxe edition, 2007
I Am ... Sasha Fierce, 2008

MOVIE AND TELEVISION CREDITS

"Carmen: The Hip-Hopera," 2001
Austin Powers in Goldmember, 2002
The Fighting Temptations, 2003
The Pink Panther, 2006
Dreamgirls, 2006
Cadillac Records, 2008
Obsessed, 2009

SELECTED HONORS AND AWARDS

With Destiny's Child

Grammy Awards (National Academy of Recording Arts and Sciences): 2000, Best R&B Song and Best R&B Vocal Performance by a Duo or Group, both for "Say My Name"; 2001, Best R&B Vocal Performance by a Duo or Group, for "Survivor"
MTV Video Music Awards (MTV): 2000, Best R&B Video, for "Say My Name"; 2001, Best R&B Video, for "Survivor"

American Music Awards: 2001, Favorite Soul/R&B Band, Duo or Group; 2002, for Favorite Soul/R&B Band, Duo or Group, and Favorite Pop/Rock Album, for *Survivor*
Image Award (NAACP): 2001, for Outstanding Duo or Group; 2005, for Outstanding Duo or Group
Soul Train Music Awards: 2001, Sammy Davis Jr. Award for Entertainer of the Year
ASCAP Pop Music Awards, Pop Songwriter of the Year (American Society of Composers and Publishers): 2002
World Music Award: 2002, for World's Best-selling Artist or Group, Pop Group, and R&B Group
Caring Hands, Caring Hearts Award (Ronald McDonald House Charities): 2005

As Beyoncé

Grammy Awards (National Academy of Recording Arts and Sciences): 2003, for Best R&B Song and Best Rap/Sung Collaboration (with Jay-Z), both for "Crazy in Love," Best Female R&B Vocal Performance, for "Dangerously in Love 2," Best Contemporary R&B Album, for *Dangerously in Love,* and Best R&B Performance by a Duo or Group with Vocals (with Luther Vandross), for "The Closer I Get to You"; 2005, Best R&B Performance by a Duo or Group with Vocals (with Stevie Wonder), for "So Amazing"; 2006, Best Contemporary R&B Album, for *B'day*
MTV Video Music Awards (MTV): 2003, Best Female Video and Best R&B Video, both for "Crazy in Love"; 2004, Best Female Video, for "Naughty Girl"; 2006, Best R&B Video (with Slim Thug and Bun B), for "Check on It"; 2007, Most Earthshattering Collaboration (with Shakira), for "Beautiful Liar"; 2009, Video of the Year, for "Single Ladies"
Soul Train Music Awards: 2004, Sammy Davis Jr. Award for Entertainer of the Year
Image Award (NAACP): 2004, for Entertainer of the Year
Broadcast Film Critics Association Awards: 2007, Best Song, for "Listen" from *Dreamgirls*
American Music Awards: 2007, International Artist Award

FURTHER READING

Books

Arenofsky, Janice. *Beyoncé Knowles: A Biography,* 2009
Biography Today, April 2001
Knowles, Beyoncé, Kelly Rowland, and Michelle Williams. *Soul Survivors: The Official Autobiography of Destiny's Child,* 2002

Periodicals

Current Biography Yearbook, 2001
Daily Variety, Dec. 1, 2006, p.2
Ebony, July 2002, p.36; Dec. 2005, p.148
Essence, Nov. 2008, p.126
Forbes, June 22, 2009, p.80
In Style, Jan. 2007, p.60; Nov. 2008, p. 286
Jet, Sep. 22, 2003, p.58; Dec. 6, 2004, p.60; Feb. 13, 2006, p.60
New Yorker, Feb. 9, 2009, p.98
New York Times, Nov. 16, 2008, p.1L
People, Oct. 6, 2003, p.87; Apr. 21, 2008
Texas Monthly, Apr. 2004, p.175; July 2009, p.54
Time, June 30, 2003, p.56
USA Today, Aug. 17, 2007, p.D14
Vanity Fair, Nov. 2005, p.336
Vogue, Apr. 2009, p.214

ADDRESS

Beyoncé
Music World Entertainment
1505 Hadley Street
Houston, TX 77002

WORLD WIDE WEB SITES

http://www.beyonceonline.com

Hillary Rodham Clinton 1947-

American Political Leader
Former U.S. Senator and Former U.S. First Lady
U.S. Secretary of State

BIRTH

Hillary Rodham Clinton was born Hillary Diane Rodham on October 26, 1947, in Chicago, Illinois. She was the first child of Hugh E. Rodham, the owner of a drapery-making business, and Dorothy Howell Rodham, a homemaker. She grew up with two brothers: Hugh Jr., three years younger, and Tony, seven years younger.

YOUTH

Rodham grew up in the middle-class suburb of Park Ridge, Illinois, northwest of Chicago. She was a good student and was active in her church and community. She was a Girl Scout and organized a fundraiser for the United Way when she was only 10. Her father stressed the importance of being thrifty, so she took her first summer job at 13, walking a few miles three days a week to supervise a local park. She also learned an interest in politics from her father, a staunch Republican who liked to debate at the dinner table; she volunteered for an anti-voter fraud effort when she was in eighth grade. She considered herself a tomboy and learned to play football and baseball from her father. She also spent a lot of time hunting, hiking, swimming, and playing cards while visiting her family's summer cabin in rural Pennsylvania.

"

"I was fortunate because as a girl growing up I never felt anything but support from my family," Clinton claimed. "There was no distinction between me and my brothers or any barriers thrown up to me that I couldn't think about doing something because I was a girl. It was just: if you work hard enough and you really apply yourself, then you should be able to do whatever you choose to do."

"

Rodham continued to excel in high school, first at Park Ridge's Maine East High School and then at Maine South, where she was moved her senior year. She belonged to the National Honor Society and student government and was named a National Merit Scholarship finalist; during the summers she worked as a lifeguard and played softball. Although she considered herself a Republican and worked for Barry Goldwater's 1964 presidential campaign, she was also very interested in civil rights and social justice, values she had learned from her mother and her Methodist faith. She often baby-sat for local migrant workers and enthusiastically participated in events organized by her youth minister, the Reverend Don Jones. These included cultural exchanges with young Hispanic and African Americans from the inner city and attendance at a 1962 speech by the civil rights leader Martin Luther King, Jr.

Rodham's parents set high expectations for her and encouraged her to succeed. "I was fortunate because as a girl growing up I never felt anything but support from my family," she claimed. "There was no distinction between me and my brothers or any barriers thrown up to me that I couldn't think about doing something because I was a girl. It was just: if you work hard enough and you really apply yourself, then you should be able to do whatever you choose to do." So Rodham never even considered that being a girl might hamper her success. In fact, she was shocked when she wrote to NASA as a teenager to volunteer for astronaut training and was told that women weren't admitted to the program. "It was the first time I had hit an obstacle I couldn't overcome with hard work and determination, and I was outraged," she wrote in her memoir *Living History.* It made her more determined to fight against discrimination of all kinds. She herself received nothing but encouragement from her own parents and teachers and was voted "most likely to succeed" by her classmates.

EDUCATION

Rodham graduated from Maine South High School in 1965 and chose to attend Wellesley College, a highly regarded women's college in Massachusetts. She earned a Bachelor of Arts degree (BA) in political science with high honors in 1969. She performed just as well outside of the classroom: she was president of the college's chapter of Young Republicans during her freshman year, and she served in the House Republican Conference in Washington DC during a summer internship. She was active in student government and was elected president her senior year. Her commencement speech to her classmates—the first ever given at Wellesley by a student—demonstrated her increasingly liberal views when she spoke of the "indispensable task of criticizing and constructive protest" and called for an end to the Vietnam War. "We feel that our prevailing, acquisitive, and competitive corporate life … is not the way of life for us," she intoned. "We're searching for more immediate, ecstatic, and penetrating modes of living." The speech earned her a profile in *Life* magazine and an invitation to join the League of Women Voters' Youth Advisory Committee. She became a Democrat sometime during this period.

After graduating from Wellesley College, Rodham entered Yale University in fall 1969 to attend law school. She was one of only 27 women in a class of 235, and she quickly became involved with activities on campus. In her first year she served on the board of editors of the alternative law journal *Yale Review of Law and Social Action* and helped mediate between groups of student protesters. During her first summer break she did research on the health and education of migrant children and her report was used by a

Bill and Hillary at Yale Law School, 1972.

U.S. Senate subcommittee. She returned to Yale determined to focus on family and children's issues. After that, she took classes at the Yale Child Study Center and worked on family law cases for the New Haven Legal Services Office. Clinton received her law degree (Juris Doctor, or JD) from Yale in 1973.

FIRST JOBS

After graduating from Yale, Rodham took a job with the Children's Defense Fund, a nonprofit group founded by Marian Wright Edelman to advocate for the rights of children. (For more information on Edelman, see *Biography Today* 1993 Annual Cumulation.) Rodham traveled the country investigating conditions in juvenile jails and uncovering discrepancies between census lists and school enrollment lists. Although she found the work rewarding, she left for an opportunity to make history.

In early 1974, Rodham accepted a position with the U.S. House Judiciary Committee. At that time, the Committee was leading an inquiry into the possible impeachment of President Richard Nixon. Rodham spent long days researching legal grounds for removal of the president, who was accused of covering up a criminal burglary of his political opponents' offices at the Watergate Hotel. The committee eventually recommended three articles of impeachment, but Nixon resigned in August 1974, before Congress could vote on them. Out of a job, Rodham decided to follow her heart to Arkansas.

"We feel that our prevailing, acquisitive, and competitive corporate life ... is not the way of life for us," Clinton said in her college commencement address. "We're searching for more immediate, ecstatic, and penetrating modes of living."

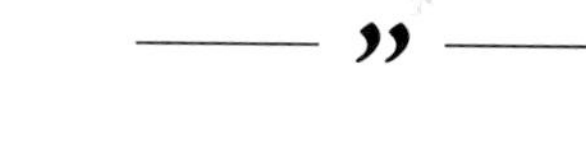

MARRIAGE AND FAMILY

Hillary Rodham first met William "Bill" Jefferson Clinton in 1970, while they were both attending Yale Law School. In her autobiography, she remembered him staring at her across the library, so she walked up and said, "If you're going to keep looking at me, and I'm going to keep looking back, we might as well be introduced." After a long courtship, the couple married on October 11, 1975. In 1980 they had their only child, Chelsea Victoria, a hedge fund consultant who has often campaigned on behalf of her mother. The Clintons maintain residences in Chappaqua, New York, and Washington, DC.

In the years since her marriage, Hillary Rodham Clinton has used several different forms of her name. When she was first married she used her maiden name, Hillary Rodham. That became a political issue after her husband was elected to office, and she was criticized for failing to take her husband's name. Since then, she has used the names Hillary Clinton and Hillary Rodham Clinton. This issue has cropped up again at various times throughout her career.

CAREER HIGHLIGHTS

Double Career in Arkansas

In 1974, shortly before she was married, Rodham had moved to Fayetteville, Arkansas, to be with her future husband. At that time, Bill Clinton was running for Congress as a Democrat. She and her family helped him campaign, but he lost to the incumbent by four percent of the vote. At the same time, Rodham became an assistant professor at the University of Arkansas School of Law. She taught classes in criminal law and also directed the school's legal aid office, where law students helped provide counsel to the poor and those in prison. In 1976 Bill Clinton ran for Arkansas attorney general, so Rodham spent much of her time assisting with his campaign. After he won the Democratic nomination—ensuring victory in a general election without a Republican opponent—she worked as field coordinator for Democrat Jimmy Carter's presidential campaign in Indiana. After Carter took office in 1977, he appointed Rodham to the board of the Legal Services Corporation, which helps fund legal aid offices across the country.

Bill Clinton's election as state attorney general meant a move to the state capital of Little Rock. Rodham left her university job and joined the Rose Law Firm, the oldest practice in the state. She was the firm's first female associate, and she later became a partner in 1979. Although some of her trials were corporate cases, she also worked for families and children. She took a case in which a family had been denied the right to adopt the foster child who had lived with them for over two years because it was against state policy. She won the case, successfully arguing that the policy was against the child's best interests, and eventually the state followed this precedent. Believing Arkansas needed an organization to promote children's rights, she and a professor of child development founded Arkansas Advocates for Children and Families soon after.

In 1978 Bill Clinton ran for governor of Arkansas and won the seat by a vote of almost two to one. Although Rodham was now First Lady of Arkansas, she continued her full schedule of legal and advocacy work. She was now a board member of the Children's Defense Fund and helped chair meetings in Washington, DC; in addition, her husband appointed her to chair the state's Rural Health Advisory Committee. Many voters, however, were perplexed by their untraditional First Lady, who kept her own name and kept working after having a baby in 1980. Bill Clinton ran for governor again in

While serving as First Lady of Arkansas, Clinton chaired the state's Educational Standards Committee, which proposed ways to improve school performance.

1980 but he lost this time, mainly due to an untimely car tag tax hike. But some observers felt that Rodham's image contributed to his defeat. She didn't fit the image that Arkansans at that time wanted in a First Lady: she was an accomplished professional in her own right; she paid little attention to her appearance, with thick glasses and long frizzy hair; and, most importantly, she hadn't changed her name when she got married. After Clinton lost the governor's race in 1980, Rodham bowed to political pressure. She took his name and had a complete makeover, exchanging glasses for contacts and styling her hair. The strategy helped, and the 1982 election returned Bill Clinton to office as governor. The family returned to the governor's mansion, where they would stay for the next 10 years.

The governor continued to depend on his wife after the 1982 election, appointing her to chair the Arkansas Educational Standards Committee, which was charged with finding ways to improve some of the nation's poorest performing schools. Under her leadership, the committee was able to push through several education reforms, including a controversial provision for teacher competency testing. Over the next few years, Bill Clinton continued to win re-election to the governor's office, while Hillary Rodham Clinton worked for Rose Law and served on the American Bar Association's Commission on Women in the Profession. She also served on the boards of nonprofit groups, including the Arkansas Children's Hospital, and of Arkansas corporations, including discount retailer Wal-Mart and frozen yogurt chain TCBY. In 1988 and 1991 the *National Law Journal* ranked her among the 100 most influential lawyers in the country.

First Lady of the United States

As a popular southern Democrat and the co-chair of the National Governors Association, Bill Clinton had first been approached about running for president before the 1988 election. He declined that year because he didn't want to spend so much time away from his young daughter, but in 1991 he announced his intent to seek the office. He formed a campaign staff, and, in an unusual move, so did Hillary Rodham Clinton, who planned to participate as fully in his presidential campaign as she had in his state ones. Her help was needed before the first primary elections in January 1992, when rumors surfaced about Bill's supposed womanizing. The accusations threatened to derail his campaign, until he and Hillary appeared on the TV news show "60 Minutes," where she defended his character and their marriage. Later, defending her own choices as a working mother and political wife, she was accused of belittling other women who had decided not to work outside the home. The Clintons' political opponents took her words out of context and accused her of being power-hungry and opposing the traditional family. Clinton found it difficult not to take the political attacks personally. As she recalled in *Living History,* "I was being labeled and categorized because of my positions and mistakes, and also because I had been turned into a symbol for women of my generation."

> *In her memoir, Clinton recalled feeling that becoming First Lady meant "I would have a 'position' but not a real 'job.' How could I use this platform to help my husband and serve my country without losing my own voice?"*

Nevertheless, many women were excited by the prospect of an energetic young couple in the White House. Aided by a majority of votes from women and young people, Bill Clinton won the 1992 election in a three-way race with Republican President George H. W. Bush and Independent Ross Perot. For Hillary Rodham Clinton, it meant new challenges. As First Lady, she had to resign from her law practice and board work. Becoming First Lady meant "I would have a 'position' but not a real 'job,'" she recalled in her memoir. "How could I use this platform to help my husband and serve my country without losing my own voice?" The Clintons decided she would serve as a full-fledged presidential advisor. She would have her own office, alongside other presidential advisors in the West Wing of the White House, and she would oversee efforts to reform the country's health care system. In support of her plan, she became the first First Lady to testify before Congress as the lead witness on a major policy initiative. Although many people found her testimony detailed and well-reasoned, others were uncomfortable with the idea of the First Lady having so much political influence.

Bill Clinton and Hillary Rodham Clinton on Inauguration Day, January 1993.

Ultimately, the Clinton plan for health care reform failed, observers have said, partially because it was too ambitious and partially because the Clintons did not make enough political alliances that might have earned the plan more support. The First Lady kept a lower political profile after this failure, focusing on smaller issues that had always been important to her, especially those involving children and families. She hosted White House Conferences on early childhood development and on child care, and contributed to efforts that eventually led to the passage of legislation. These laws included the Children's Health Insurance Program, which provided health care for poor children; the Family and Medical Leave Act, which ensured employees with new babies or sick relatives the right to unpaid leave; and the Adoption and Safe Family Act of 1997, which encouraged moving foster children to adoption. Clinton also began communicating more directly with the American public. She began writing a syndicated newspaper column in 1995, and released a book on children and families, *It Takes a Village,* in 1996.

Although the First Lady was sometimes a polarizing figure at home, she was very popular abroad and frequently traveled on behalf of the United States as an official representative. Clinton made visits to ordinary women part of

Clinton testifying before the U.S. House of Representatives Energy Committee, which was holding hearings on health care reform.

her schedule, looking for programs that could improve women's lives. Her speech at the Fourth United Nations World Conference on Women, given in China in 1995, inspired women worldwide. Decrying abuses against women in China and all over the world, Clinton concluded, "If there is one message that echoes forth from this conference, let it be that human rights are women's rights and women's rights are human rights, once and for all." To continue assisting women worldwide in developing their political and economic skills, Clinton founded the Vital Voices Democracy Initiative in partnership with Madeleine Albright, Secretary of State during Bill Clinton's second term. Vital Voices has since become an important nonprofit, non-governmental organization that holds conferences and training sessions for women and advocates for human rights, including laws against human trafficking and programs to support people with HIV and AIDS.

During her husband's presidency, Clinton became both a figure of controversy and of sympathy. The controversy came from the Whitewater investigation, named after a parcel of Arkansas land. The Clintons had invested in the project with a developer who later ran a shady savings and loan company. Although the Clintons lost money on their investment, they were accused of using their political influence to assist the developer, then covering up their involvement. Although an initial report cleared them of any wrongdoing, there was an extended investigation that was promoted by their political enemies. The First Lady was called to testify before a grand jury in 1996, and the Senate also investigated her actions. These further investigations concluded there was no evidence to show any criminal wrongdoing, but they also revealed that the President had conducted an inappropriate sexual relationship with a young intern. Again, Hillary Clinton was called to defend her husband to save his political career, and again she demonstrated her support. By October 1998 her approval ratings were near 70 percent, although many questioned why such a strong woman would stay with a husband who had cheated on her. Clinton addressed the issue in her memoir: "All I know is that no one understands me better and no one can make me laugh the way Bill does. Even after all these years, he is still the most interesting, energizing, and fully alive person I have ever met."

U.S. Senator from New York

As the Clinton presidency was nearing its end in 1999, many Democrats believed Hillary Clinton's strong public profile and policy experience would make her an excellent candidate for public office. Clinton had thought of running a university or foundation after leaving the White House and was hesitant to stay in the harsh media spotlight as a political candidate. Finally, however, she decided it wasn't enough to talk about empowering women when she could make a difference by holding an office of her own. In 1999 she decided to target the open Senate seat in New York, although she had never lived there and would be running against Rudy Giuliani, the popular mayor of New York City. She and the President bought a house in Chappaqua, and she began a "listening tour" of New York state. During her campaign, she emphasized improving education and helping boost the upstate economy, outside of New York City. When Giuliani dropped out of the race to deal with prostate cancer, Clinton ended up running against Congressman Rick Lazio, whose aggressive campaign tactics turned off many voters. Clinton won the race 55 to 43 percent, becoming the first sitting First Lady to be elected to office in her own right.

Although her critics expected her to barge ahead with big policy issues in the Senate, Clinton showed she had learned from her early days in the White House. She started out slowly, getting acquainted with her fellow Senators and limiting her legislative proposals to bills designed to help economically depressed upstate New York. "The importance of building relationships among colleagues, of trying to create coalitions behind the issues that you are championing, was not something I ever had much insight into until I was elected and started serving in the Senate," she noted. After the terrorist attacks of September 11, 2001, brought down the World

Senator Clinton in the halls of the U.S. Senate.

Trade Center in New York City, Clinton focused on getting disaster aid to the city. By the end of 2001, she had introduced or co-sponsored some 70 pieces of legislation and had won the respect of colleagues in both parties.

Perhaps Clinton's most important vote during her first term was when she joined with Republicans and 22 other Democrats in October 2002 to authorize President George W. Bush to take military action against Iraq. Although she later criticized how the administration waged the Iraq War, she noted that "I don't regret giving the president authority because at the time it was in the context of weapons of mass destruction, grave threats to the United States, and clearly, Saddam Hussein had been a real problem for the international community for more than a decade." During her first Senate term, Clinton also served on several Senate committees, including those for the Budget; Environment and Public Works; Health, Education, Labor and Pensions; and the Armed Services. When she joined the Armed Services Committee in 2003, many believed it was to gain foreign policy experience for a future presidential run of her own. She was one of the country's most visible Democrats, and when she became chair of the Senate Democratic Steering Committee in 2003, she became a leading voice in setting policy for the party. Clinton, however, said her new assignment was merely part of serving the citizens of New York, who had a vested interest in homeland security and national defense after 9/11.

Although many thought (and others hoped) Clinton would run for president in 2004, she ruled out the possibility early on and declared she had no interest in joining the Democratic ticket as vice president. "I'm having the time of my life," she said of her work as a senator. "I pinch myself every morning." She was easily re-elected to the Senate in 2006, beating her Republican challenger by a vote of more than two to one. She had spent $34 million, more than any other Senate candidate that year, a move some believed was designed to raise her national profile for the 2008 presidential election. There was no question Clinton was the biggest fundraiser in the Democratic Party, able to appear almost anywhere in the country and bring in political contributions. She was popular outside the party, as well: her 2003 memoir *Living History* sold over 1.5 million copies in the U.S. during its first year alone.

Making History as a Presidential Candidate

In early 2007, Clinton announced her intention to run for president. She was considered the immediate frontrunner in a field that also included fellow Senators Barack Obama of Illinois and John Edwards of North Carolina (a candidate for vice president in 2004), as well as New Mexico Governor Bill Richardson. Not only did Clinton have greater name recognition and experience, she also performed well in early candidate debates and raised the most money for her campaign. For many Democrats, it was a difficult choice between her, the first strong female candidate for President, and Barack Obama, the first strong African-American contender. Clinton emphasized her "deep experience over the last 35 years" and stated "I wouldn't be in this race and working as hard as I am unless I thought I am uniquely qualified at this moment in our history to be the president we need."

The lead-up to a presidential election is a long process. The Democratic and Republican parties each hold a series of special elections in states around the country to determine who will win the party's nomination for president. These special elections, called primaries and caucuses, begin in winter of the election year and continue through the spring. During this time, the candidates from a single party vie against each other to win votes and win each state's election. In late summer, each party holds a convention to officially select their nominees for president and vice president. The battle between parties' candidates continues until the election in November, followed by the inauguration in January.

Clinton suffered a setback in the first caucus of the year, where she came in third behind Obama and Edwards. Observers thought her campaign was over, but she came back to win the next primary after sharing an emotional moment with voters about why she kept going despite the challenges of campaigning. "I listened to you, and in the process I found my own voice," she later commented. Still, the contest became increasingly competitive, as Obama's message of change resonated more with voters than Clinton's emphasis on experience. The Clinton campaign focused more on primaries, which are conducted by secret ballot, effectively leaving the caucus states, where open votes are held after meetings, to the Obama camp. On February 5—called Super Tuesday because over 20 state elections were held—Clinton and Obama earned nearly the same number of votes and delegates, although Obama carried more states. His lead kept growing over the next few months, but Clinton stayed competitive, hoping that she could gain enough votes from superdelegates—important officials in the Democratic Party—to win the nomination.

In the 2008 presidential race, Clinton said, "I wouldn't be in this race and working as hard as I am unless I thought I am uniquely qualified at this moment in our history to be the president we need."

After the final primary on June 3, 2008, however, it was clear that Barack Obama would clinch the Democratic presidential nomination. In conceding the race, Clinton referred to making history as the first woman to win a presidential primary and also to the number of votes she had received from her supporters: "Although we weren't able to shatter that highest, hardest glass ceiling, this time, thanks to you, it has about 18 million cracks in it and the light is shining through like never before." She quickly gave her endorsement to Obama, and many Democrats hoped that he might select Clinton as his vice-presidential running mate. Although Obama chose Delaware Senator Joseph Biden instead, Clinton continued to campaign around the country on behalf of the Democratic ticket, appearing at more than 200 rallies and fundraisers for more than 80 candidates.

After Obama won the presidential election in November 2008, many speculated Clinton might seek a role in his cabinet, a Supreme Court position, or even the governorship of New York. She told reporters she looked forward to returning to the Senate. "I'm not interested in just enhancing my visibility," she remarked. "I'm interested in standing on the South Lawn of the White House and seeing President Obama signing

Clinton on the campaign trail, campaigning for president in Charleston, West Virginia, March 2008.

into law quality affordable health care for everybody, and voting in a big majority for clean, renewable energy and smarter economic policies. That's what I'm all about, and I'm going to use every tool at my disposal to bring it about." Nonetheless, few were surprised when the President-elect announced he had chosen Clinton to become his Secretary of State, the person responsible for implementing U.S. foreign policy and the highest ranking position in the president's cabinet.

U.S. Secretary of State

Clinton was hesitant to take the job at first; she wanted to get back to the Senate and work on issues important to her and her constituents, like health care. Eventually, Obama persuaded her to say yes. "It came down to my feeling that, number one, when you president asks you to do something for your country, you really need a good reason not to do it," she explained. "Number two, if I had won and I had asked him to please help me serve our country, I would have hoped he would say yes. And finally, I looked around our world and I thought, you know, we are in just so many deep holes that everybody had better grab a shovel and start digging out." She was easily confirmed by the Senate, by a vote of 94 to two.

The Secretary of State is part of the Executive branch of the government. She advises the President on foreign policy and supervises the nation's rela-

As Secretary of State, Clinton has many different roles: advising President Barack Obama (shown here in the Oval Office) on issues related to foreign affairs and national security; participating in a ceremonial tree planting in Nairobi, Kenya; talking to female artisans about how they have achieved economic self-sufficiency in Mumbai, India.

tionships with other countries. She also works to ensure the security of the United States. As Clinton took office, there were many challenges around the world facing the U.S.: military conflicts in Iraq and Afghanistan; nuclear proliferation in Iran and North Korea; a trade imbalance with a rapidly growing China; and the need to work with other countries on issues of economics and security. But Clinton was undaunted by these challenges, as she told the Senate confirmation committee: "I don't get up every morning thinking only about the threats and dangers we face. With every challenge comes an opportunity to find promise and possibility in the face of adversity and complexity. Today's world calls forth the optimism and can-do spirit that has marked our progress for more than two centuries."

Clinton immediately identified five strategies to advance American foreign policy: first, appoint special envoys for hot spots and issues; second, engage in dialogue with adversaries; third, establish aid and development "as a core pillar of American power"; fourth, coordinate civilian and military efforts, as in Iraq and Afghanistan; and fifth, use the power of America's example to inspire the world. She got off to a fast start on these goals by naming special envoys for Afghanistan and Pakistan, Iran, North Korea, and the Israeli-Palestinian conflict. She also got more funds earmarked for the State Department, to add staff and increase foreign aid.

In her first year as Secretary of State, Clinton was a visible advocate for American interests. Although surgery for a broken elbow hampered her for a couple of weeks, she still traveled thousands of miles and made trips to more than two dozen countries, including Mexico, China, Indonesia, India, and several countries in Africa, Europe, the Middle East, and the Caribbean. She continued the policy she began as First Lady of meeting everyday citizens, holding town hall meetings to answer questions about American policy and even appearing on an Indonesian television show. As she said in a 2009 speech to the Council on Foreign Relations: "In every country I visit, I look for opportunities to bolster civil society and engage with citizens, whether at a town hall in Baghdad [Iraq]—a first in the country; or appearing on local popular television shows that reach a wide and young audience; or meeting with democracy activists, war widows, or students." Clinton had a lower profile at home, leading the media to speculate she was being underused by the Obama administration, but she was enjoying her new job leading the State Department. "I feel very much in the center of helping to devise the policies, carry out the policies, pick the people who will implement the policies," she said. "I see the president every week. We spend a lot of time talking."

As for her own presidential aspirations, Clinton would be 69 years old in 2016, the next election needing a new Democratic candidate (since Obama

"I always find those moments of grace, and I always see something that makes it important enough to keep going," Clinton said. "When somebody says that if it hadn't been for me they aren't sure their son would have survived because I fought with some insurance company to get them health care, I think, well, that's what politics is supposed to be about. I love that, and that's why I do what I do."

will presumably run again in 2012). By adding experience as Secretary of State to her résumé, some observers believe, she would make an even more formidable candidate the second time around. Clinton remarked in 2009 that "I have a very committed attitude toward the job I'm doing now," so another run is "not anything that is at all on my radar screen." Whether she runs or not, however, Clinton is clearly dedicated to a life of public service. Despite the challenges, "I always find those moments of grace, and I always see something that makes it important enough to keep going," she said. "When somebody says that if it hadn't been for me they aren't sure their son would have survived because I fought with some insurance company to get them health care, I think, well, that's what politics is supposed to be about. I love that, and that's why I do what I do."

HOBBIES AND OTHER INTERESTS

Her busy schedule leaves Clinton little time for hobbies, although she is known to enjoy ballet, art, and sculpture. A devout Methodist, she makes time for prayer groups and Bible study. In order to facilitate charitable giving, she cofounded the Clinton Family Foundation with her husband and daughter in 2001. Since then, the Foundation has donated more than $7 million to various charities, churches, hospitals, and arts and education organizations, including more than $2 million in 2008 alone.

SELECTED WRITINGS

It Takes a Village, 1996

Dear Socks, Dear Buddy: Kids' Letters to the First Pets, 1998 (compiler)

An Invitation to the White House: At Home with History, 2000 (with Carl Anthony)

Living History, 2003

SELECTED HONORS AND AWARDS

National Humanitarian Award (National Conference of Christians and Jews): 1987 (with Bill Clinton)
Named to 100 Most Influential Lawyers in the U.S. list (*National Law Journal*): 1988 and 1991
Albert Schweitzer Leadership Award (Hugh O'Brian Youth Foundation): 1993
Friend of Family Award (American Home Economics Association): 1993
Claude D. Pepper Award (National Association for Home Care): 1993
Distinguished Service, Health Education and Prevention Award (National Center for Health Education): 1994
Special Achievement Award (Hispanic Public Corporation): 1994
Living Legacy Award (Women's International Center): approx. 1994
Grammy Award (National Academy of Recording Arts and Sciences): for best spoken word album, 1997, for *It Takes a Village*
United Arab Emirates Health Foundation Prize (World Health Assembly): 1998
Lifetime Achievement Award (Children of Chernobyl Relief Fund): 1999
Mother Theresa Award (Government of Albania): 1999
German Media Prize: 2004
President's Vision and Voice Award (American Women's Medical Association): 2005
National President's Award (Reserve Officers Association): 2005
Energy Leadership Award (Energy Efficiency Forum): 2006
Trailblazer Award (Vital Voices Global Partnership): 2009
Margaret Sanger Award (Planned Parenthood Federation of America): 2009

FURTHER READING

Books

Bernstein, Carl, *A Woman in Charge,* 2007
Clinton, Hillary Rodham. *Living History,* 2003

Periodicals

Atlantic, Nov. 2006, p.56
Chicago Tribune, Jan. 21, 2007
Christian Science Monitor, Mar. 10, 2003, p.1
Current Biography Yearbook, 2002, 2009
Economist, Feb. 9, 2008, p.28
Newsweek, Jan. 21, 2008, p.60; Dec. 29, 2008, p.44
New Yorker, Oct. 13, 2003, p.63

New York Times, Sep. 6, 1995, p.A10; July 19, 1998, p.1; May 23, 2006, p.1; June 8, 2008, p.A1; Dec. 3, 2008, p.A20; Feb. 5, 2009, p.12; Apr. 18. 2009, p.A4; May 2, 2009, p.A5; July 16, 2009, p.A1
New York Times Magazine, May 23, 1993
People Magazine, Dec. 28, 1998, p.104; July 1, 2002, p.101
Time, Nov. 17, 2008, p.80
USA Today, June 11, 2009, p.1A
Wall Street Journal, June 4, 2008, p.A1
Washington Post, Sep. 8, 2005, p.A12; July 16, 2009, p.A3; Aug.13, 2009, p.A8

Online Articles

http://www.CNN.com
(CNN, "Hillary Rodham Clinton Scores Historic Win in New York," Nov. 8, 2000; "Hillary Clinton: No Regret on Iraq Vote," Apr. 21, 2004; "Hillary Clinton: I Said No, At First, to Secretary of State Job," June 7, 2009)
http://www.firstladies.org
(National First Ladies Library, "First Lady Biography: Hillary Clinton," no date)
http://topics.nytimes.com/topics/reference/timestopics/index.html
(New York Times, "Hillary Rodham Clinton," multiple articles, various dates)
http://topics.newsweek.com/people/politics
(Newsweek, "Hillary Rodham Clinton," multiple articles, various dates)
http://www.time.com
(Time, "The 2009 Time 100 Finalists,"
http://www.whitehouse.gov/about/first_ladies/hillaryclinton
(White House, "Hillary Rodham Clinton," no date)
http://www.clintonpresidentialcenter.org/the-administration/hillary-rodham-clinton
(William J. Clinton Presidential Center, "Hillary Rodham Clinton," no date)

ADDRESS

Hillary Clinton
U.S. Department of State
2201 C Street NW
Washington, DC 20520

WORLD WIDE WEB SITES

http://www.state.gov/secretary

Eran Egozy 1971-
Alex Rigopulos 1970-

American Video Game Designers

Creators of the Award-Winning Video Games *Guitar Hero* and *Rock Band*

EARLY YEARS

Eran B. Egozy was born in Israel, a Middle Eastern country located on the eastern shore of the Mediterranean Sea. His family moved to the U.S. when he was 12 years old. As a child, Egozy was interested in music. He learned to play the clarinet, a woodwind instrument most often used in classical and jazz music.

Alexander P. Rigopulos was born in Massachusetts and grew up in the Boston area. When he was three years old, his parents bought a Magnavox Odyssey, the first video game console made for use with home televisions. Rigopulos loved playing video games, and he soon became interested in the computer technology that made the games work. He also enjoyed playing the drums.

EDUCATION

Egozy attended the Massachusetts Institute of Technology (MIT), where he studied electrical engineering and music. As a classical clarinet player, Egozy often performed as a soloist with the MIT Symphony Orchestra, the MIT Chamber Music Society, and MIT's Gamelan Galak Tika orchestra. ("Gamelan" means "to hammer" and is the name for percussion groups that perform the traditional music of the Indonesian islands of Bali and Java.) Throughout his years at MIT, he studied music and technology at the MIT Media Lab, a research department that focuses on developing new technologies. In 1995, Egozy earned both a Bachelor of Science degree (BS) in electrical engineering and computer science and a Master of Science degree (MS) in electrical engineering and computer science.

"Playing music is, I think, one of the most fundamentally joyful experiences that life has to offer," Rigopulos declared. "Just about everyone tries at some point in their life to learn to play music: piano lessons as a kid, guitar lessons as a teenager, or whatever."

Rigopulos also attended MIT, and he was a student there at the same time as Egozy. Rigopulos studied music with a focus on composition, keyboards, and percussion. He sang with the MIT Concert Choir and was among the first members of MIT's Gamelan Galak Tika orchestra. He also played the drums in a local rock band that was known for performing songs by groups like Led Zepplin and Pink Floyd. Rigopulos earned a Bachelor of Science degree (BS) in humanities in 1992. He also stayed at MIT as a graudate student, where he studied computer music at the MIT Media Lab. Rigopulos earned a Master of Science degree (MS) in computer music in 1994.

At the MIT Media Lab, Egozy and Rigopulos were assigned to share an office. Although their paths had crossed before, they did not know each

Egozy and Rigopulos first became partners while students at Massachusetts Institute of Technology (MIT), while working at the Media Lab.

other very well before then. Egozy and Rigopulos soon discovered that they shared an interest in combining music and technology. They both loved playing music, and they wanted everyone to be able to do that too, regardless of talent or experience. "Playing music is, I think, one of the most fundamentally joyful experiences that life has to offer," Rigopulos declared. "Just about everyone tries at some point in their life to learn to play music: piano lessons as a kid, guitar lessons as a teenager, or whatever."

They realized that learning to play music was difficult for most people, and it took a lot of time to master a musical instrument. "The overwhelming majority of people give it up after six months or a year in frustration, just because it's too difficult to learn to play music the old-fashioned way," Rigopulos explained. "Consequently, this profound joy that comes from making music is only accessible to this tiny percentage of the people of the world." Egozy and Rigopulos began to work together to find a way for technology to make it easier for people to share the fun of making music.

"When we handed someone a game controller and said they would be making music, as opposed to playing a game, they were skeptical, self-conscious," Rigopulos admitted. "But if we said here is a game, they were happy to dive in. So we learned that we needed to present this experience as a video game if we were to realize our secret, clandestine mission to make musicians out of people."

According to Egozy, "Alex and I got interested in the question, 'How do you get average people to be able to express themselves musically by using technology?'" He and Rigopulos created several different computer programs that allowed people to make music by pressing buttons or moving a mouse or joystick. These early programs became very popular at the Media Lab, and were often used as examples of the new technologies that were being developed at MIT.

When their time at the Media Lab was coming to an end, Egozy and Rigopulos decided to continue working together outside MIT. "We joked around about how no one would hire us, so we started a company," Egozy said. "We wanted to keep doing what we were doing. But it wasn't just that; it was that we saw the appeal, the sparkle in people's eyes and the smile that came to their faces when they touched this thing and were able to express themselves. We thought, 'Wow, we actually have something here.'"

CAREER HIGHLIGHTS

In 1995, Egozy and Rigopulos founded Harmonix Music Systems with one goal in mind: to help non-musicians have the experience of making music. "We created this company to try to invent new ways to give music-loving non-musicians—the millions of passionate air guitarists in the world—[a chance] to play music," explained Rigopulos. "Our mission was to show non-musicians how it feels when you finally get to the other side. And hopefully, to inspire them to start making music the old-fashioned way."

As the creators of the wildly popular and critically acclaimed video games *Guitar Hero* and *Rock Band*, Egozy and Rigopulos are seen as video gaming pioneers. Harmonix is recognized as one of the leading developers of music-oriented video games in the world. But success did not come quickly or easily. It took ten years of hard work, frustration, and many disappointments before Harmonix released its first successful product.

Getting Started

When Egozy and Rigopulos worked together at MIT, their goal was to create computer programs called prototypes. These prototypes served as examples—they showed how technology could help people make music. At MIT, it was enough that their prototypes worked and that people were impressed with the technology. However, Egozy and Rigopulos quickly learned that the business world is very different from MIT's research labs. Impressive technology was not enough anymore, and it turned out to be very difficult to turn their ideas into something that people would buy. Rigopulos said, "We had this naïve assumption that if we made something that had a lot of 'Wow, how'd they do that?' factor, it would sell."

Harmonix struggled with one failure after another in its first few years. Rigopulos now refers to that time as "the dark ages." Egozy and Rigopulos were creating new technology and pushing the capabilities of computer programming, but they were not making a profit from their work. "I don't mean we were earning no money," Rigopulos explained. "I mean we had near zero revenue. We were raising money and spending it, building stuff that no one actually wanted to pay for." Even with the financial support of investors, Harmonix nearly went out of business more than once. Rigopulos said, "We were on the brink of death, I don't know, 10 times."

Harmonix released its first official product in 1997. *The Axe* was a computer program that turned the movements of a mouse or joystick into musical notes, similar to the early prototypes that Egozy and Rigopulos created at MIT's Media Lab. *The Axe* was not a video game; there were no goals to reach or points to be scored. Egozy and Rigopulos thought that creating improvised music was entertaining enough on its own. "We weren't really thinking about video games," Rigopulos stressed. "We were making interactive music-making, free-form creative experiences." At the time it was released, *The Axe* was a completely new idea for computer software. "You couldn't really explain it to anyone," Egozy conceded. "People would actually have to physically sit down and try it to see what it was doing. We could guide them through it, and then they'd smile and we'd know they got it, but of course that is no way to market a product on a large scale."

The innovative new technology of *The Axe* was praised by computer software reviewers. A music critic for the *Boston Globe* called *The Axe* "armchair entertainment at its best," while a writer for *Keyboard* magazine said that "using the program is as easy as it gets." In spite of the impressive technology and positive reviews, ultimately only about 300 copies of *The Axe* were sold. In 1998, some of the technology created for *The Axe* was used for a new music-making exhibit at Disney World's Epcot Center theme park. The exhibit allowed park visitors to create music just by waving their hands in the air. Although the technology was admired by people working in the computer industry, the lack of commercial success was another disappointment for Harmonix. Egozy and Rigopulos moved on to develop new software that they hoped more people would want to buy.

Creating Video Games

In 2001, Harmonix released *Frequency*, its first music video game. The release of a second music game, *Amplitude,* followed in 2003. Harmonix hoped that combining music-making and game play would attract more buyers. In both games, players create music while navigating through futuristic environments, with eye-dazzling computer graphics and songs from such artists such as David Bowie, No Doubt, Pink, and Weezer. *Frequency* and *Amplitude* were also the world's first online multiplayer music games. "*Frequency* and *Amplitude* introduced the notion of game play," Egozy explained. "That was another big turning point. The root of this whole thing was combining music with joysticks, which was really a gaming thing, but it took us about four years to realize that we should actually be building a game." At first, it was hard to encourage people to try to make music. "When we handed someone a game controller and said they would be making music, as opposed to playing a game, they were skeptical, self-conscious," Rigopulos admitted. "But if we said here is a game, they were happy to dive in. So we learned that we needed to present this experience as a video game if we were to realize our secret, clandestine mission to make musicians out of people."

A game reviewer for IGN.com called *Frequency* an "amazingly good game" that is easy to play, even for non-gamers. *Amplitude* was nominated for the 2003 Best PS2 Game award, named by *Rolling Stone* magazine as one of the four Best Console Games of 2003, and listed as one of IGN.com's 2003

Amplitude *and* Frequency, *two early offerings from Harmonix, were their first video music games.*

Reader Top 10 PS2 games. Despite such high praise from the press and the video gaming industry, neither game sold very well. Harmonix was still attracting fans among video game professionals, but had yet to impress video game players.

Harmonix's next attempt at creating a successful product was *Karaoke Revolution*, a series of singing games released from 2003 to 2005. Here, Rigopulos describes the design process for *Karaoke Revolution:* "We took a step back and said, 'Well, what kind of game can we create that has incredibly broad, mainstream appeal so even people who don't consider themselves 'gamers' would be willing to pick up this game and give it a try? How can we turn the tide and help expand people's understanding of what music gaming is, and put it on the map as a mainstream category?' That was a big part of the conception of *Karaoke Revolution*."

> *When it was released in 2005,* Guitar Hero *was advertised as "a shrine to the glory of rock guitar and a fiendishly addictive fusion of music and gameplay."*

Karaoke Revolution won the 2003 Gaming Innovation of the Year award from *Electronic Gaming Monthly* and was named *Time* magazine's No. 1 Video Game of 2003. It was also nominated for 1UP.com's 2003 Game of the Year award. A video game reviewer for GameDaily.com called *Karaoke Revolution* "fantastic" and "the perfect game for anyone who celebrates the joys of music." Sales of Karaoke Revolution were good, and Harmonix finally earned its first profits—10 years after starting out.

In 2004, Harmonix released *EyeToy: AntiGrav*, its only non-music video game. An extreme sports hoverboarding game, *EyeToy: AntiGrav* was the world's first video game in which players moved their whole body to control a video game character. The game helped to define the new "physical gaming" technology, which was just beginning to emerge at that time. At first, physical gaming was unfamiliar and strange to most video game players. There were also some problems with the camera that was used to sense a player's movements. Reviews of *EyeToy: AntiGrav* were mixed, with criticism focusing on the camera's occasional inconsistent motion sensing. A staff game reviewer for GameSpot.com praised the game's "inventive design" and "totally immersive experience," but complained that the game's technology was not yet able to track accurately the full-body motions required to control the game. The staff of 1UP.com said the motion control worked "amazingly well" but noted that it was difficult to play the game in certain situations, for example if the room's lighting was too dim or too bright for the camera. Once again, Harmonix had pushed the capabilities of video gaming technology almost beyond the limits of what was possible.

Guitar Hero

In 2005, Egozy and Rigopulos were contacted by RedOctane, a small company that made such video game hardware as the special mats used for the home version of the popular *Dance Dance Revolution* video game. RedOctane wanted to produce a new version of a Japanese video game called *Guitar Freaks*. RedOctane proposed that Harmonix would create a guitar-based music game, and RedOctane would manufacture the plastic guitars needed to play it. Egozy and Rigopulos were initially skeptical, doubting that this was a good idea. "Any rational analysis told you this game was not going to be successful," Rigopulos later said. He and Egozy weren't sure how well it would sell, because the guitar that was included with the game increased the price as well as the space needed to display the larger box on store shelves. But the idea did present an opportunity to create a new kind of music-making game for non-musicians. Rigopulos eventually decided that Harmonix should go into partnership with RedOctane. "Even though it wasn't going to make us any money, it was a game we were going to love to make."

Released in 2005, *Guitar Hero* was advertised as "a shrine to the glory of rock guitar and a fiendishly addictive fusion of music and gameplay." To play the game, players strum and push colored buttons on a small plastic guitar to match the rhythm and tempo of the game's music, indicated by colored dots that appear on the screen. Much to everyone's surprise, *Guitar Hero* became an overnight sensation. It became the runaway hit of the 2005 holiday shopping season, selling so fast that most stores could not keep the game in stock. *Guitar Hero* sold faster than any other video game in history, reaching $15 million in sales in its first two months—more than Harmonix had earned in the previous 10 years combined. The game also quickly became a pop culture phenomenon, attracting celebrity fans, appearing on magazine covers, and being featured in television shows. Egozy said, "We had no idea it would become this huge." In an interview with *Game Developer* magazine, Harmonix team members said, "We on the *Guitar Hero* team are all somewhat astonished that we actually got paid to make this game....It was pure fun from beginning to end."

In addition to being a huge hit with game players, game critics and industry professionals also loved *Guitar Hero*. A reviewer for *Official PlayStation Magazine* called the game "ridiculously awesome," while *Inc.* magazine

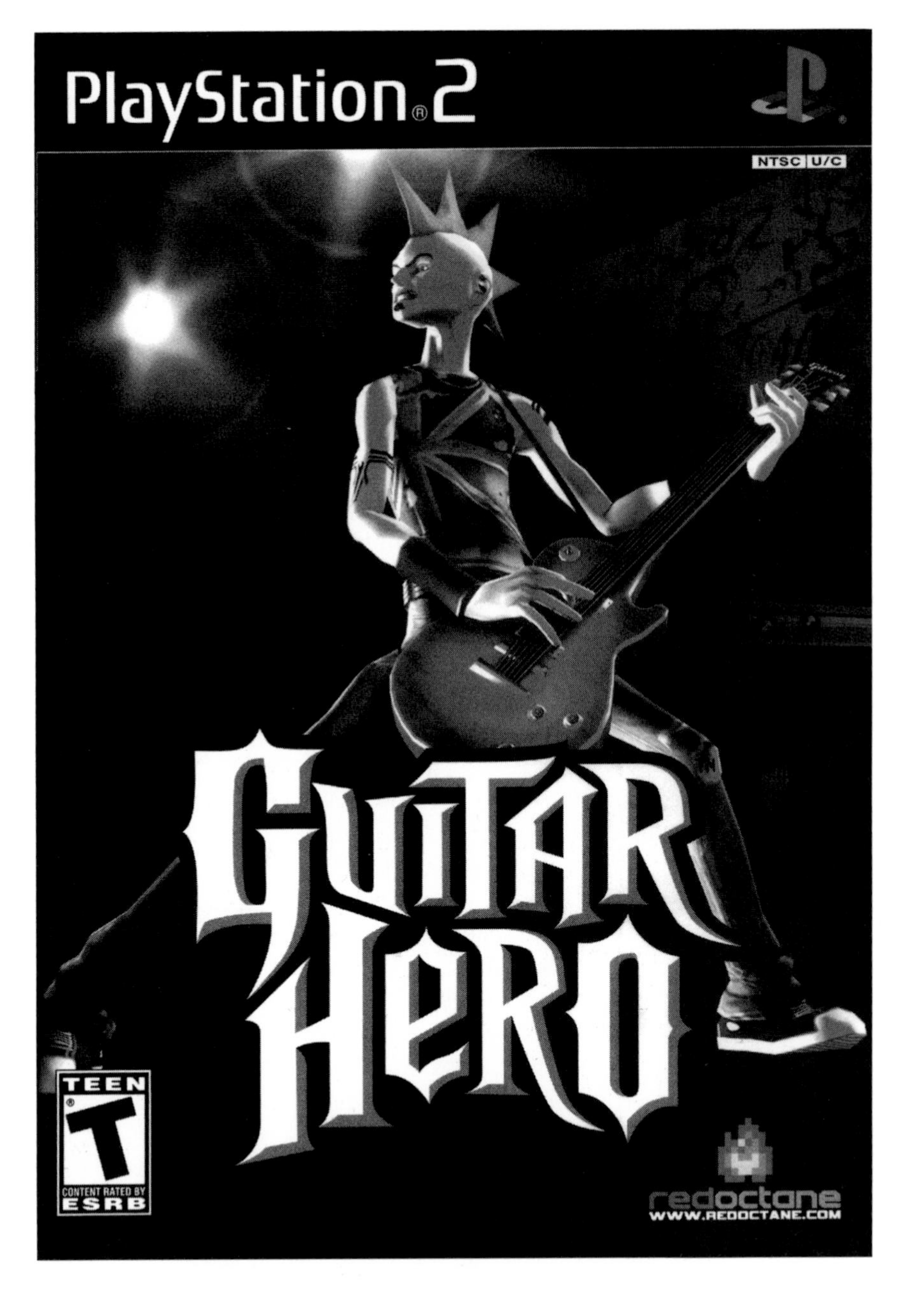

Egozy and Rigopulos had their first big hit with Guitar Hero.

said *Guitar Hero* is "shockingly fun." *Newsweek* praised *Guitar Hero* as a "cultural and high-tech phenomenon that is changing the way we interact with music." *Guitar Hero* won five Interactive Achievement Awards, two Game Developers Choice Awards, and was nominated for Game of the Year by both organizations. *Guitar Hero II*, released in 2006, continues to be ranked as one of the Top 10 games for PlayStation 2.

The phenomenal success of *Guitar Hero* and *Guitar Hero II* also captured the attention of large media entertainment companies looking to invest in new products. In 2006 Harmonix was purchased by Viacom, a large media conglomerate that also owns MTV. Around the same time, RedOctane was acquired by Activision, a major video game publisher. Because RedOctane owned the right to publish *Guitar Hero*, the game went with the sale. Activision and Viacom were fierce competitors and were unwilling to collaborate on the development of future games. Because of this conflict, Harmonix was no longer allowed to develop games for the *Guitar Hero* series. So once again, Egozy and Rigopulos turned their attention to new projects.

Egozy has credited their success to their early years working at the MIT Media Lab. "MIT really instills in you the notion of wanting to do original work, and not being satisfied by copying what someone else has done, and building new things. I think it's been sewn into the fabric of the company that being creative and original and innovative is just the way to do things. It's just kind of second nature. You look at the products we've made, and we're always trying to do new things in new ways."

Rock Band

Although Harmonix could no longer release games under the *Guitar Hero* name, Egozy and Rigopulos still held patents on the technology used in the game. This gave them the right to use *Guitar Hero*'s computer programs to create new games based on the same concept. The result was *Rock Band*, a complete music performance simulation game that expanded *Guitar Hero* by combining guitar, bass guitar, drums, and singing in one game. *Rock Band* allows simultaneous play by up to four people, with each player using small replica instruments to play or sing their part of a song. Players can join together to form a band in the same room, or they can connect to others through an online version of the game. *Rock Band* can also be played by fewer people, with the computer filling in the parts of the missing instruments.

Rock Band was released in 2007 and quickly became another phenomenal success for Harmonix. As the first multiplayer music performance game, *Rock Band* was a hit with music fans, video game players, and reviewers. *Inc.* magazine called it "the most realistic rock-star simulation yet" and praised Harmonix for producing "another monster hit." *Wired* magazine called *Rock Band* "the ultimate music game," and *Time* said it was "the best party game ever made." *Rock Band 2* was released in 2008 and featured more music tracks and additional downloadable content. By the end of that year, more than seven million copies of *Rock Band* games and 26 million downloadable songs for the game had been sold.

In 2009, a new version of *Rock Band* was released focusing on the music of The Beatles. The British rock band first became famous in the 1960s and went on to become one of the world's most influential and successful rock bands of all time. "I think particularly younger players or listeners probably don't have an appreciation of just the sheer magnitude of the phenomenon, that there was nothing before and frankly, has not been anything like it since," Rigopulos stressed. "There are no rock bands in the world today that are the same kind of magnitude or phenomenon that The Beatles were."

The Beatles: Rock Band game spans the group's entire career, including performances on stage and in the recording studio. The usual computer animation found in *Rock Band* is combined with film recordings of the real band members, creating a unique visual experience that is new for music performance video games. Another innovation for music games is the introduction of multiple singing parts in *The Beatles: Rock Band.* As Rigopulos explained, "For the singing game play in our previous games, we've always focused on a single singer singing a single part, but harmonies are such a critical aspect of The Beatles music that this was an area we felt we had to innovate in this game."

Egozy and Rigopulos are widely credited with being groundbreaking leaders in their field, and in 2008 they were both included in *Time* magazine's list of the 100 most influential people in the world. "People talk about music games as a new category of games, but for me, music games are a new category of musical entertainment," Rigopulos said. "We make music games, but we consider it to be music first and games second. We really consider what we do in this category to be making new kinds of music experiences and to let people experience music in a new way. Our goal with

Scenes from Rock Band, *which expanded on the success of* Guitar Hero *by allowing multiple players at one time.*

Rock Band has always been to go beyond making music games and create a true music platform."

Egozy and Rigopulos are widely recognized as innovators in the field of video gaming. In 2009, they received the Game Developers Choice Pioneer Award, considered by many industry professionals to be the highest honor in game development. Egozy has credited their success to their early years working together as graduate students at the MIT Media Lab. "MIT really instills in you the notion of wanting to do original work, and not being satisfied by copying what someone else has done, and building new things. I think it's been sewn into the fabric of the company that being creative and original and innovative is just the way to do things. It's just kind of second nature. You look at the products we've made, and we're always trying to do new things in new ways."

HOBBIES AND OTHER INTERESTS

Egozy enjoys playing the clarinet and has been a member of Boston's Radius Ensemble chamber music group since 2001. He is a frequent participant in the Apple Hill Chamber Music Festival in New Hampshire. He also mentors entrepreneurs through the MIT Enterprise Forum, the MIT 100K competition, and other organizations.

In his spare time, Rigopulos plays the drums and sometimes performs in the Boston area with his brother in their band, Yeast.

Through Harmonix, Egozy and Rigopulos support music education and enrichment programs for young people. The Harmonix Music and Youth Initiative provides free music education to young people in the greater Boston area. Harmonix supports Music Drives Us, an organization that promotes music education throughout New England. Harmonix also works with the Starlight Foundation to bring music opportunities to children facing chronic and life-threatening illnesses.

HONORS AND AWARDS

Editor's Choice Award (IGN.com): 2001, for *Frequency*
Gaming Innovation of the Year (*Electronic Gaming Monthly*): 2003, for *Karaoke Revolution*
Number 1 Video Game of 2003 (*Time*): 2003, for *Karaoke Revolution*
Best Console Game of 2003 (*Rolling Stone*); 2003, for *Amplitude*
Family Game of the Year (Academy of Interactive Arts and Sciences): 2006, for *Guitar Hero;* 2007, for *Guitar Hero II*; 2008, for *Rock Band*

Interactive Achievement Award (Academy of Interactive Arts and Sciences): 2006, for *Guitar Hero*
Outstanding Achievement in Game Design (Academy of Interactive Arts and Sciences): 2006, for *Guitar Hero*
Outstanding Innovation in Gameplay Engineering (Academy of Interactive Arts and Sciences): 2006, for *Guitar Hero*
Best Hardware/Peripheral (Game Critics Award): 2007, for *Rock Band*
Best of Show (Game Critics Award): 2007, for *Rock Band*
Best Social/Casual/Puzzle (Game Critics Award): 2007, for *Rock Band*
Outstanding Achievement in Soundtrack (Academy of Interactive Arts and Sciences): 2007, for *Guitar Hero II*; 2008, for *Rock Band*; 2009, for *Rock Band 2*
100 Most Influential People in the World (*Time*): 2008
Entertainment Marketers of the Year (Advertising Age): 2008, for *Rock Band*
Outstanding Achievement in Gaming (Academy of Interactive Arts and Sciences): 2008, for *Rock Band*
Pioneer Award (Game Developers Choice Awards): 2009

FURTHER READING

Periodicals

Inc., Oct. 2008, p.124
Newsweek, Jan. 29, 2007; Jan. 7, 2008, p.78; May 5, 2008
Rolling Stone, Mar. 18, 2009
Time, Apr. 29, 2008
Wired, Sep. 14, 2007

Online Articles

http://arstechnica.com
(Ars Technica, "King of Rock: Ars Talks to Harmonix CEO Alex Rigopulos," Jan. 15, 2009)
http://blastmagazine.com
(Blast, "E3 2009: Harmonix CEO Alex Rigopulos interviewed by *Blast*," June 3, 2009)
http://www.gamecritics.com
(GameCritics, "Interview with Alex Rigopulos," Mar. 31, 2004)
http://freakonomics.blogs.nytimes.com/2009/01/13/the-guitar-hero-answers-your-questions
(New York Times, "The *Guitar Hero* Answers Your Questions," Jan. 13, 2009)
http://www.newsweek.com/id/134023
(Newsweek, "Rock-and-Roll Fantasy: Harmonix, Creator of *Rock Band* and *Guitar Hero*, Is Changing Videogames," May 5, 2008)

http://www.portfolio.com/culture-lifestyle/goods/gadgets/2007/09/17/Harmonix-Profile
(Portfolio, "The Guitar Heroes," Sep. 17, 2007)
http://www.rollingstone.com
(Rolling Stone, "The RS 100 Agents of Change," Mar. 18, 2009)
http://www.technologyreview.com/article/22213
(Technology Review, "Music for the Masses," Mar./Apr. 2009)

ADDRESS

Eran Egozy
Alex Rigopulos
Harmonix Music Systems, Inc.
625 Massachusetts Ave., 2nd Floor
Cambridge MA 02139

WORLD WIDE WEB SITE

http://www.harmonixmusic.com

Neil Gaiman 1960-

British Comic Book Creator and Author of Books for Children and Young Adults
Creator of *The Sandman, Coraline,* and the Newbery Award-Winning *The Graveyard Book*

BIRTH

Neil Richard Gaiman was born on November 10, 1960, in Porchester, England. He was the oldest child of David and Sheila Gaiman. David was a director of a vitamin and supplement company and Sheila was a pharmacist. Neil has two sisters, Claire and Lizzy.

YOUTH

Gaiman's childhood was full of the pleasures of books. He learned to read at age four and was soon devouring everything he could get his hands on; he claims to have read every book in the youth section of his local library. "I was a reader," he later said. "I loved reading. Reading things gave me pleasure. I was very good at most subjects in school, not because I had any particular aptitude in them, but because normally on the first day of school they'd hand out schoolbooks, and I'd read them—which would mean that I'd know what was coming up, because I'd read it."

Gaiman's early influences included everything from classic fantasy writers to the operas of Gilbert and Sullivan. Among his favorite authors were J.R.R. Tolkien, C.S. Lewis, and Lewis Carroll, whose works he read throughout his childhood. He first read Tolkien's *Lord of the Rings* at his school library. The library only had the first two volumes of the trilogy, and he took them out over and over. When he won the school English prize and the school reading prize in the same year, he got the third Tolkien volume and a collection of English poetry. Gaiman vividly remembers receiving Lewis's seven-volume series *The Chronicles of Narnia* for his seventh birthday. He was captivated by Lewis's prose style and the narrative voice in the work. "I admired his use of parenthetical statements to the reader, where he would just talk to you.... I'd think, 'Oh, my gosh, that is so cool! I want to do that! When I become an author, I want to be able to do things in parentheses.' I liked the power of putting things in brackets." Another much-loved title was Carroll's *Alice in Wonderland,* which Gaimain called "a favorite title forever. Alice was default reading to the point where I knew it by heart." In all this mix of classic children's literature, he had time for comics, too. *Batman* was an early favorite.

"

"I was a reader," Gaiman recalled. "I loved reading. Reading things gave me pleasure. I was very good at most subjects in school, not because I had any particular aptitude in them, but because normally on the first day of school they'd hand out schoolbooks, and I'd read them—which would mean that I'd know what was coming up, because I'd read it."

"

Deciding to Become a Writer

Gaiman knew from a very young age that he wanted to be a writer. In an

Gaiman signing autographs for a young fan in China.

interview with his youngest daughter, Maddy, he said that his first composition was a poem, which he created at the age of three and which was transcribed by his mother. When he was 15, he told his school career counselor that he wanted to be a writer, specifically of "American comic books." The counselor recommended he become an accountant.

EDUCATION

Gaiman attended Ardingly College, a local grammar school, from the ages of 10 to 14, then went on to Whitgift School, the equivalent of an American high school, from the ages of 14 to 17. At 17, he decided to leave school and begin his life as a writer.

CAREER HIGHLIGHTS

In a career that has already spanned over 20 years, Neil Gaiman has become one of the finest fantasy writers of his generation, an author who has made comics and graphic novels an accepted literary art form. In addition, he won the 2009 Newbery Medal, as the author of the finest work of American literature for children. He has published works in an astonishing variety of genres, including novels, short stories, poetry, comics, graphic novels, screenplays, music, and journalism, and for a wide variety of read-

> *When he was 15, Gaiman told his school career counselor that he wanted to be a writer, specifically of "American comic books." The counselor recommended he become an accountant.*

ers, from fantasy and comic book fans to adults, young adults, and young children.

One of the interesting aspects of Gaiman's work is the ways in which he has recreated many of his works in new genres and new formats. For example, he first wrote a famous comic book series *The Sandman,* then later created a graphic novel series also titled *The Sandman,* then published *The Absolute Sandman,* an enhanced collection of the original comic books. Similarly, he wrote *Stardust* as a comic book, then reimagined it as a novel. His beloved work *Coraline* was first published as a young adult novel, then recreated as a graphic novel, and then later made into a movie.

Early Journalism

Gaiman first made his living as a journalist, writing book and film reviews for English newspapers and magazines. He was also sending off his own short stories to publishers and receiving nothing but rejection letters. He was determined to stay in journalism, however, because he was writing about the world he wanted to be a part of, the world of fantasy and science fiction. "I'm a journalist," he told himself at the time. "As of right now, I'm a freelance journalist specializing in science fiction, fantasy, and horror in the world of publishing, because that's what I want to understand."

Gaiman began pitching ideas to publishers, saying he had an interview with a well-known fantasy writer, like Gene Wolfe, and hoping they would buy the piece. And they did. Gaiman also took on a book project, a biography on the rock group Duran Duran. He has claimed the book was bad, but the band was so popular the first printing sold out. Convinced he was going to be awash in royalty payments, Gaiman went to the publisher's office only to discover that they'd gone bankrupt.

Then, Gaiman got a job offer from a magazine, *Penthouse,* that publishes nude photos. He thought long and hard about it. It would be a steady source of income, and by then he had a wife and two young children to support. But he knew that was the wrong path to take, and he turned the job down. "I had this amazing, complete confidence in my ability, totally unjustified," he recalled. Then he found the right path.

First Comics

In 1987, Gaiman began work on his first comic, *Violent Cases,* which was illustrated by his long-time collaborator and friend, Dave McKean. As in most of Gaiman's work, it depicts alternate worlds: the real world and a dream, or parallel, world. The comic drew the interest of DC Comics, the powerhouse that publishes such blockbusters as *Superman* and *Batman.* They asked Gaiman and McKean for another comic, and the duo produced *Black Orchid.* Karen Berger, head of the Vertigo line at DC Comics, saw potential in the work, and she offered Gaiman a great opportunity: to produce a new comic series, based on an old DC character, the Sandman, but reimagined by him. The result is considered one of the greatest comics of all time, the work that paved the way for the success and respectability of the graphic novel.

The Sandman

Gaiman's *Sandman* comic originally appeared in 75 monthly installments, 24 pages each, published by DC Comics from December 1988 to March 1996. Beginning with the earliest issues, Gaiman's concept was clear: his Sandman, known as Dream or Morpheus, was not a gumshoe type of detective, as he was first envisioned. Instead, he is the mystical, brooding ruler of the dream world, who has been around for eternity and is part of a family of godlike beings known as the Endless. Each of them represents some aspect of humanity, with names like Destiny, Death, Destruction, Desire, Despair, and Delirium. When readers first encounter Dream, he is being held captive by an evil human. But what could have been a conventional revenge story takes on a different aspect early on.

In *Sandman,* there are a number of characters who've fallen prey to a sleeping sickness and who live in their dreams; Dream can enter, and affect, those dreams. These and other themes are presented in a series that is flavored with myth and fairy tale, encompassing a timeline that covers centuries, with characters of a depth and richness not before seen in comics. Episodes feature real figures, like Shakespeare and Marco Polo; figures from religion and myth, like the Devil and Cain and Abel; and startling new creations. There's an emotional richness, too, that brought many new readers to the world of comics. *Sandman* was the first comic that was popular with female readers, who became part of Gaiman's devoted following.

Gaiman is always quick to note that he was part of a collaborative team that created *Sandman,* including a writer, artist, letterer, inker, colorist, and cover artist. The writer, Gaiman, provided the story line, dialogue, and art

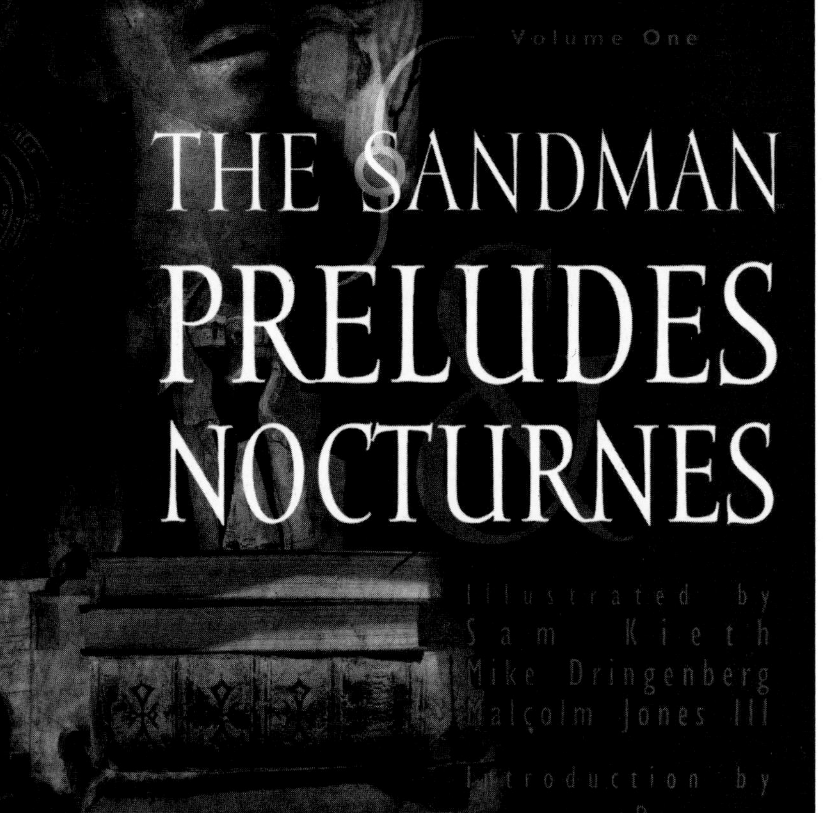

The first volume of The Sandman, *the graphic novel series that Gaiman based on his ground-breaking comic books.*

direction. The artists, Sam Kieth, Mike Dringenberg, and Malcolm Jones III, created the sketches and placement of the panels. Todd Klein did the lettering, and Robbie Busch was the colorist. The *Sandman* covers were done by Dave McKean. Together, they set a new standard for verbal and visual expression in comics. The series won many awards and a wide following among readers, critics, and other authors.

Sandman was also an important "first" in many ways. Gaiman was able to gain partial control of the character, which normally stays in the hands of the publisher. He was also able to end the comic series, which he did in 1996, while launching separate works based on some of Dream's siblings. Gaiman also published works based on *Sandman* in several other genres. He created a graphic novel series based on the comics that was one of the earliest attempts at the new genre. It's interesting to note that in early response to the series, several writers thought that graphic novels would never be accepted by the reading community; Gaiman has proven how wrong they were. *Sandman* has also appeared in a third format, the *Absolute Sandman* series, a complete multivolume book set of the comic book series.

While still working on *Sandman,* Gaiman and his family decided to move to the United States. They settled outside of Minneapolis, near his wife's family, in 1992.

Expanding His Range

Around this time, Gaiman decided to spread his wings to create works in different formats and for different ages. He wrote several novels for adults, beginning with *Good Omens,* a collaborative novel he wrote with Terry Pratchett in 1990 that became a bestseller. While continuing to produce work in other genres, Gaiman added to his adult novel line with *American Gods* in 2001 and *Anansi Boys* in 2005, both critical and popular successes.

Gaiman has also created screenplays for television and movies. In 1996, he wrote a fantasy TV series for the BBC in England called *Neverwhere.* It tells the story of a man whose life is changed when he stops to help an injured girl on a London sidewalk and is plunged into an alternate world below the streets of the "real" city. Gaiman developed a novel from the series, which he published in 1997 and which went on to become a bestseller. He's also written a screenplay for a movie version, which was purchased by Jim Henson Productions, a company run by the family of the famous creator of the Muppets. The Jim Henson company also produced the 2005 movie *MirrorMask,* whose screenplay was written by Gaiman. It also tells a story about an alternate world, this time featuring a 15-year-

Gaiman's first book for younger readers.

old girl, Helena, who is drawn into a strange and dangerous fantasy world. After writing the movie script, Gaiman went on to create two works based on that movie: a picture book for young adult readers and a heavily illustrated book containing the movie screenplay, art work, and story boards from the film.

In addition to these works, Gaiman wrote the screenplay for the English-language version of *Princess Mononoke,* the 1999 anime classic by the famed Japanese artist Hayao Miyazaki, as well as the screenplay for an adaptation of the famous epic *Beowulf.* And he wrote and directed a movie entitled *A Short Film about John Bolton* in 2002. He's produced many different screenplays based on his novels and comics, some of which have been produced and some of which are still under consideration or in revision.

Works for Younger Readers

In 1997, Gaiman published his first work for young readers, *The Day I Swapped My Dad for Two Goldfish,* with illustrations by his frequent collaborator Dave McKean. The story describes how a little boy, left in his distracted father's care, is visited by a friend showing off his two goldfish. The boy wants them badly and makes a proposition to his friend: he'll trade his dad for the goldfish. The deal takes place and havoc ensues, until his mother comes home and sets things right. Gaiman says the book was inspired by his son, Michael. When told to go to bed one night as a little boy, Michael said, "I wish I didn't have a Dad. I wish I had … a goldfish!" Such knowing insights into children and their ways make this one of Gaiman's most delightful works for young people.

Gaiman's next book for young readers was *The Wolves in the Walls* (2003). It was inspired by his daughter Maddy, who woke up one night from a nightmare claiming there were wolves in the walls. With illustrations by Dave McKean, the book describes what happens when a girl named Lucy tries to convince her family that there is a pack of menacing wolves lurking in the house. They don't believe her until the wolves come out of the walls. Lucy is full of courage and outwits the wolves in this scary and funny tale. In 2008, Gaiman published *The Dangerous Alphabet.* This picture book, originally created as a kind of Christmas card, presents a story told in 26 alphabetical lines. It features two children with a treasure map who sneak out of their house and into a world of monsters and pirates beneath the city.

"You can do so many things with fantasy," Gaiman explained. "At a rock-bottom level, you can concretize a metaphor. Part of it is that, if you're a writer, you can play God. This is my world, you are welcome to come, but I get to call the shots, and I won't be embarrassed to pull in anything I need or want."

In 2009, Gaiman published several new books for young readers. *Blueberry Girl* is a beautiful picture book based on a poem that Gaiman originally wrote for his friend, musician Tori Amos, when she found out she was going to have a baby girl. It is full of all the blessings that parents everywhere want for their beloved children. *Crazy Hair,* inspired in part by his own wild hair, and by his daughter Maddy's comments on it, is another recent favorite. Illustrated by Dave McKean, it features a girl named Bonnie who attempts to bring some control to her friend's "crazy hair." Another recent work, *Odd and the Frost Giants,* reflects Gaiman's love for myth, especially Norse myth. Set in Norway, the book features a boy named Odd who meets some fantastical creatures during his quest to help the Norse gods.

Books for Teens and Young Adults

Some of Gaiman's most beloved works are those written for teenagers and young adults. His first work for this audience was the 1998 young adult novel version of *Stardust,* based on his earlier comic book of the same name. This novel is set in England many years ago, in the town of Wall. There's a young man, Tristan Thorn, who wants to impress the girl he loves, Victoria Forester. He claims that he will catch a falling star and bring it back to her. He climbs the wall for which the town is named, and, as often happens in Gaiman's tales, he enters another world, the land of Faerie, which is full of magic and fantastic adventure. The book inspired a movie of the same name, which came out in 2007 and brought Gaiman even more fans.

Coraline

Gaiman came to the attention of many teen readers for the first time in 2002, with the publication of his novel *Coraline*. Like most of Gaiman's works, it features parallel worlds, alike but unalike, with dangers and delights. Coraline Jones is a young girl who moves into a house her family shares with several strange and unusual neighbors. She is an only child, and a lonely one, too. Her self-involved parents sit at their computers working hours every day and have little time for their curious child. One day, while exploring the new house, Coraline discovers a door in the wall. She goes through it and finds a world much like her own, but distinctly different. Her parents are there, but her "other mother" is nurturing and kind and loves to cook Coraline mountains of delicious food. Her father, too, has all the time in the world for his little girl.

At first, Coraline thinks of her new world as a dream come true. But it's strange, too, in ways that are weird and inexplicable. Her "dream" mother changes: instead of nurturing, she becomes witchlike and controlling and tries to force Coraline to stay on "her" side of the house. Soon, Coraline realizes both she and her "real" parents are in great danger. It takes all of her courage and ability to win back her real world from the menacing forces of the "other" world.

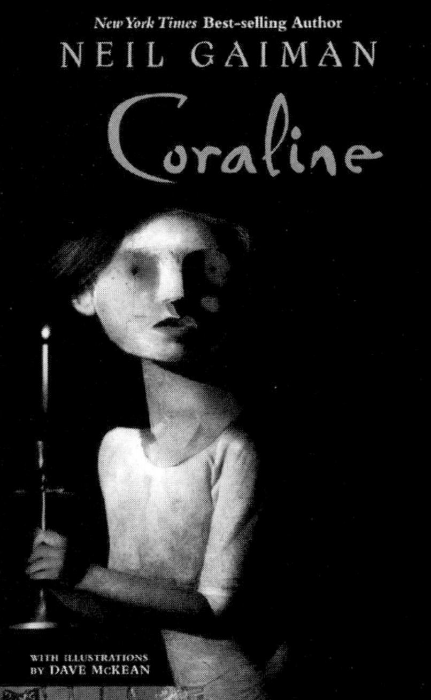

Gaiman's novel Coraline *was turned into an animated movie and a graphic novel, too.*

The novel was a great success and won Gaiman many awards and many new readers, both young and old. *Coraline* became even more popular in 2009 with the release of a film based on the novel. The film version of *Coraline* was directed by Henry Selick, who also directed Tim Burton's *Nightmare Before Christmas*, and was shot in 3-D stop motion animation, a technique that for many enhanced the novel's atmosphere of weirdness and adventure.

More Books for Teens and Young Adults

In 2005, Gaiman published *MirrorMask*. This funny and scary fantasy tale tells the story of a 15-year-old girl, Helena, who works for her family circus. She wants to run away and join the "real" world, to live an ordinary life. Instead, she ends up in a magical dream world filled with strange, fantastic, and dangerous creatures. Helena must fulfill a quest to escape the alternate world and return home to her own life. Like many of Gaiman's works, *MirrorMask* appeared in several formats. He first wrote the screenplay for the 2005 movie of the same name, which he followed with a picture book for young adults based on the movie.

"

Asked to defend fantasy as a genre for children's literature, especially in Coraline, *Gaiman said this: "The whole point of* Coraline *is summed up in the little quote from G. K. Chesterton I put at the beginning of the book. It reads, 'Fairy tales are more than true: not because they tell us that dragons exist, but because they tell us that dragons can be beaten.'"*

"

Another work enjoyed by young adults is *M Is for Magic* (2007), a collection of 10 short stories plus a poem. Here, Gaiman created stories that seem to rely on the familiar but are all entirely different, with unexpected twists and turns. All showcase his vivid imagination, his storytelling skill, and his knowledge of what will appeal to teen readers. In *InterWorld* (2007), which Gaiman wrote with Michael Reeves, a young boy named Joey Harker discovers that his world exists within an alternate world, the "Altiverse," where there's infinite number of Earths in infinite dimensions. After Joey develops the power to travel between these dimensions, he discovers that he's in danger, because others—the armies of magic and science—want this special power, too. Joey, and the others like him, band together to protect their world.

MirrorMask *came out in several different forms: first Gaiman wrote the movie screenplay, then he wrote a novel for teens and also created an illustrated film script.*

The Graveyard Book

In 2008, Gaiman published *The Graveyard Book*. It begins with a scene of terror: a family is murdered in their beds by a killer. Only the family toddler escapes death. Unaware of the carnage taking place, he scoots out of his crib, climbs down the stairs, and steals through the open front door. From there, he wanders down the street and into the local graveyard. Once again, Gaiman creates a brilliant parallel world: a community of the dead, with their own society and rituals. The ghosts who make the graveyard their home take in the little boy and decide to raise him. Mr. and Mrs. Owens become his father and mother, and he is renamed Nobody Owens, called Bod for short.

> *Gaiman is a fierce defender of the rights of authors to publish what they wish without censorship. "The First Amendment is something that I think is really, really cool," he argued. "I'm from England. There is no First Amendment there, no guaranteed freedom of speech."*

The ghosts and otherworldly creatures that inhabit the graveyard are devoted to Bod and his safety. They range in age and type from a Roman officer who died while conquering Britain, to a witch who was drowned in the 1500s, to the mysterious Silas, neither alive nor dead, who becomes Bod's guardian and greatest influence. Silas knows that the murderer is still after Bod, and his menacing presence casts its shadow over the entire novel.

The book chronicles Bod's life from his toddler years to his early teens and is in many ways a "coming-of-age" novel. Gaiman stated that his greatest influence in writing the book was Rudyard Kipling's *Jungle Book,* in which wild animals take in and raise a young human. He also recalled his first vision of the book: in the mid-1980s, he and his family were living in a tall, narrow house in England, with no yard where his son Michael, then a toddler, could play. Instead, Gaiman would take Michael to the local graveyard. He remembers having a brief glimpse of what would become *The Graveyard Book* as his son rode his tricycle up and down the cemetery.

But it took the urging of his daughter Maddy to get the book done. Gaiman had written what would become Chapter Four, "The Witch's Headstone," and he read it to her. She responded in the way that every author wants to hear: "What happens next?" Gaiman resolved to find out, and the result was *The Graveyard Book*, which became a best seller and a critical success.

Winning the Newbery Medal

In January 2009, Gaiman learned that he had won the prestigious Newbery Medal, given every year by the American Library Association to the most distinguished work of American literature for children. He was overwhelmed, and as a creature of the modern age of communication, he sent out a tweet that contained some foul language. That, and the novel's dark atmosphere and themes of murder and death, led some concerned adults to wonder whether the book was appropriate for young readers. On his web site for young people, Gaiman addressed the issue. In answer to the question, "Are you ever worried that you will introduce a world to children that is too horrific for them to handle?" his reply is simply, "No."

Speaking about His Ideas

Gaiman is frequently asked why he's devoted to the genre of fantasy. Recently, he said this: "You can do so many things with fantasy. At a rock-bottom level, you can concretize a metaphor. Part of it is that, if you're a writer, you can play God. This is my world, you are welcome to come, but I get to call the shots, and I won't be embarrassed to pull in anything I need or want." Asked to defend fantasy as a genre for children's literature, especially in *Coraline,* he said this: "The whole point of *Coraline* is summed up in the little quote from G. K. Chesterton I put at the beginning of the book. It reads, 'Fairy tales are more than true: not because they tell us that dragons exist, but because they tell us that dragons can be beaten.'"

Gaiman is a fierce defender of the rights of authors to publish what they wish without censorship. He is a passionate member of the Comic Book Legal Defense Fund, which defends authors in censorship cases. "The First Amendment is something that I think is really, really cool," he argued. "I'm from England. There is no First Amendment there, no guaranteed freedom of speech." Now that he lives in America, he works hard to keep writing and speech free.

Advice to Young Writers

Gaiman is frequently asked for advice on writing by his young fans. Here's a sampling of his replies: "Write. Finish things. Keep writing."

Gaiman's novel The Graveyard Book *won the Newbery Medal, given to the most distinguished book of American literature for children.*

MARRIAGE AND FAMILY

Gaiman married Mary Therese McGrath on March 14, 1985. They have three children: Michael, born in 1983; Holly, born in 1985, and Madeleine, called Maddy, born in 1994. The Gaiman family moved to the outskirts of Minneapolis, Minnesota, in 1992, where they lived in a house the author describes as looking like something "out of a Charles Addams cartoon." He and Mary are now divorced, but are still friendly and live next door to each other in rural Wisconsin.

Gaiman loves being a dad, and his children have inspired his work for years. He says of his daughter Maddy, "It's been fun doing things like *Coraline* and having a daughter to try them out on. It's simply lovely having somebody who thinks this stuff is fun. From Maddy's point of view, really, the cool thing is the fact that I know Lemony Snicket, that she got to have dinner with Daniel Handler, the fact that R.L. Stine says hello. I am now cool."

NEIL GAIMAN'S JOURNAL

Gaiman keeps in close contact with his many fans through his blog, a journal that is accessible through his web site. He has hundred of thousands of fans worldwide, and his site receives thousands of hits each day, as they follow his constant creative activity.

SELECTED WRITINGS

Comics

Violent Cases, 1987 (comic book)
Black Orchid, 1988 (comic book)
The Sandman, 1988-97 (comic book)
The Books of Magic, 1989 (comic book)
The Books of Magic, 1993 (comic book collection)
Stardust, 1997-99 (comic book)
Stardust, 1998 (comic book collection)
The Absolute Sandman, Vols. 1-4, 2006-08 (comic book collection)

Graphic Novels

The Sandman, 1991-2003
Preludes & Nocturnes, 1991
The Doll's House, 1991
Dream Country, 1991
Season of Mists, 1992
A Game of You, 1993

Fables & Reflections, 1993
Brief Lives, 1994
World's End, 1995
The Kindly Ones, 1996
The Wake, 1996
Endless Nights, 2003
Coraline, 2009

Books for Children and Young Adults

The Day I Swapped My Dad for Two Goldfish, 1997
Stardust, 1998
Coraline, 2002
The Wolves in the Walls, 2003
MirrorMask, 2005
InterWorld, 2007 (with Michael Reaves)
M Is for Magic, 2007
The Dangerous Alphabet, 2008
The Graveyard Book, 2008
Blueberry Girl, 2009
Crazy Hair, 2009
Odd and the Frost Giants, 2009

Novels for Adults

Good Omens, 1990 (with Terry Pratchett)
Neverwhere, 1997
American Gods, 2001
Anansi Boys, 2005

Other

Neverwhere, 1996 (screenplays for television series)
A Short Film about John Bolton, 2002 (author and director)
MirrorMask, 2005 (screenplay)
Beowulf, 2007 (screenplay; with Roger Avary)

HONORS AND AWARDS

International Horror Guild Award: 1995, for *Angels & Visitations: A Miscellany*
Defender of Liberty Award (Comic Book Legal Defense Fund): 1997
Mythopoeic Fantasy Award (Mythopoeic Society): 1999, for *Stardust*
Geffen Award (Israeli Society for Science Fiction and Fantasy): 2000, for *Stardust*; 2002, for *American Gods*; 2004, for *Smoke and Mirrors*

Bram Stoker Award (Horror Writers Association): 2000, for *The Sandman: The Dream Hunters;* 2002, for *American Gods;* 2003, for *Coraline;* 2004, for *The Sandman: Endless Nights*
Hugo Award (World Science Fiction Society): 2002, for *American Gods;* 2003, for *Coraline;* 2004, for *A Study in Emerald;* 2009, for *The Graveyard Book*
Locus Award (*Locus* magazine): 2002, for *American Gods;* 2003 (two awards), for *Coraline* and *October in the Chair;* 2004 (three awards), for *The Sandman: Endless Nights, A Study in Emerald,* and *Closing Time;* 2009, for *The Graveyard Book*
Nebula Award (Science Fiction and Fantasy Writers of America): 2002, for *American Gods;* 2003, for *Coraline*
Best Book for Young Adults (American Library Association): 2003, for *Coraline;* 2009, for *The Graveyard Book*
Best Book of the Year (*Publishers Weekly*): 2003, for *Coraline*
Bulletin Blue Ribbon Book Award (*Bulletin of the Center for Children's Books*): 2003, for *Coraline*
Children's Choice Award (International Reading Association): 2003, for *Coraline;* 2004, for *Wolves in the Walls*
Notable Children's Book Award (American Library Association): 2003, for *Coraline;* 2009, for *The Graveyard Book*
British Science Fiction Award: 2003, for *Coraline;* 2004, for *The Wolves in the Walls*
British Fantasy Award for Best Novel/ August Derleth Award (British Fantasy Society): 2006, for *Anansi Boys*
Top Ten Fiction Books (*Time* magazine): 2008, for *The Graveyard Book*
Newbery Medal (American Library Association): 2009, for *The Graveyard Book*

FURTHER READING

Books

Wagner, Hank, Christopher Golden, and Stephen R. Bissette. *Prince of Stories: The Many Worlds of Neil Gaiman,* 2008

Periodicals

American Libraries, Mar. 2009, p.49
Booklist, Aug. 2002, p.1949
Children & Libraries, Spr. 2003, p.26
Horn Book, July/Aug. 2009, p. 351
Los Angeles Times, Sep. 3, 1995, Magazine, p.14
New York Times, Jan. 27, 2009, p.C1

Publishers Weekly, July 28, 2003, p.46
Reading Today, Apr./May 2009, p.19
School Library Journal, Mar. 2009, p.30
Time, Aug. 6, 2007, p.62
Voice of Youth Advocates, Dec. 2002, p.358
Washington Post, Nov. 1, 1995, p.B1

Online Periodicals

http://www.avclub.com
(AV Club, "Neil Gaiman," Sep. 28, 2005)
http://www.bookpage.com/0308bp/neil_gaiman.html
(BookPage, "Crossing Over: Adult Author Neil Gaiman Enters the World of Children's Books," 2003)
http://www.indiebound.org/author-interviews/gaimanneil
(IndieBound, "Neil Gaiman Interview," Aug. 1, 2005)
http://www.januarymagazine.com/profiles/gaiman.html
(January Magazine, "January Interview: Neil Gaiman," Aug. 2001)
http://www.locusmag.com/2005/Issues/02Gaiman.html
(Locus Magazine, "Neil Gaiman: Different Kinds of Pleasure," Feb. 2005)
http://www.wildriverreview.com/worldvoices-neilgaiman.php
(Wild River Review, "Myth, Magic, and the Mind of Neil Gaiman," Aug. 2007)

ADDRESS

Cat Mihos
for Neil Gaiman
4470 Sunset Blvd. #339
Los Angeles, CA 90027

WORLD WIDE WEB SITES

http://www.neilgaiman.com
http://www.mousecircus.com (Gaiman's site for younger readers)
http://www.harpercollins.com/Author/Browse.aspx

Hugh Jackman 1968-

Australian Actor, Singer, and Dancer
Award-Winning Star of Movies and Musical Theater
Plays Wolverine in the *X-Men* Movie Series

BIRTH

Hugh Michael Jackman was born on October 12, 1968, in Sydney, New South Wales, Australia. His mother, Grace Watson, and his father, Chris, were both British. The family moved from England to Australia when Jackman's father, an accountant, accepted a job transfer a year before Jackman was born. Jackman has two older sisters and two older brothers.

YOUTH

Jackman grew up in an upper-class suburb of Sydney, the largest city in Australia. He liked to spend time outdoors, and he went to the beach almost every day. His family often went on camping trips and traveled extensively throughout Australia. As a child, Jackman dreamed of visiting other countries and far-away places. "I used to spend nights looking at atlases," he recalled. "I decided I wanted to be a chef on a plane. Because I'd been on a plane and there was food on board, I presumed there was a chef. I thought that would be an ideal job." Jackman also liked to sing and dance in variety shows that he made up for his family.

When Jackman was eight years old, his parents divorced and his mother moved back to England. She eventually married again and later gave birth to his half-sister. Jackman didn't see his mother very often after she left Australia, and he had almost no relationship with her for many years. His father did not remarry, and he raised Jackman and his brothers and sisters as a single father.

"It wasn't until I was 22 that I ever thought about my hobby being something I could make a living out of," Jackman commented. "As a boy, I'd always had an interest in theater. But the idea at my school was that drama and music were to round out the man. It wasn't what one did for a living. I got over that. I found the courage to stand up and say, 'I want to do it.'"

EDUCATION

Jackman attended an exclusive school for boys in Sydney. He liked to participate in musical productions at school, beginning when he was about five years old. His interest in theater continued into his teen years—although he has admitted that by that time he was partly motivated by the chance to meet girls. Jackman also played rugby on the school's team. (Rugby is a ball game that is roughly similar to American football, though the rules of play are different. Rugby involves a lot of physical contact, but players don't wear protective gear.)

After completing high school, Jackman began studying journalism at the University of Technology in Sydney. He planned to become either a television news reporter or a talk show host. While working on his journalism degree, Jackman decided on a whim to take a drama class at the Actors

Center in Sydney. He enjoyed it so much that he abandoned journalism and began to study acting full time. "It wasn't until I was 22 that I ever thought about my hobby being something I could make a living out of," Jackman explained. "As a boy, I'd always had an interest in theater. But the idea at my school was that drama and music were to round out the man. It wasn't what one did for a living. I got over that. I found the courage to stand up and say, 'I want to do it.'" He applied and was accepted to study acting at the prestigious Western Australian Academy of Performing Arts, one of Australia's premiere schools for the arts. Jackman graduated from the Academy in 1994.

CAREER HIGHLIGHTS

Jackman's career has been one of the most varied among current performers. He has been described as "a singer, a dancer, an actor, and an action figure" and "an absolute gentleman" by those who have worked with him over the years. Though he is perhaps best known for his portrayal of mutant superhero Wolverine in the *X-Men* movie series, Jackman has found success in stage plays, musical theater, television, and movies of almost all genres. He has hosted numerous performing arts award ceremonies, including the televised broadcasts of the Tonys and the Oscars. Though his projects are not always commercially successful, Jackman has earned critical acclaim and multiple awards and honors for his performances.

Getting Started as an Actor

Jackman has worked almost continuously as an actor since graduating from the Academy in 1994. In fact, on the night of his final Academy graduation performance, he got a phone call offering him a starring role on "Corrrelli," a 1995 Australian television crime drama. Jackman accepted the part. "I was technically unemployed for about 13 seconds," he later recalled. On "Correlli," his costar was Deborra-Lee Furness, a well-known Australian TV actress. The characters' on-screen romance soon developed into a real-life relationship for the two actors, ultimately leading to marriage. "Correlli" lasted only one season. Jackman said of his time on the show, "Meeting my wife was the greatest thing to come out of it."

After "Correlli," Jackman was cast in a 1996 production of the musical *Beauty and the Beast* in Melbourne, Australia, even though at that time he couldn't sing very well. "I guess they liked me enough to send me away for singing lessons," he speculated. "Either that or they were desperate to fill this role." The lessons paid off, and critics praised Jackman as one of the most promising newcomers in musical theater. His success in *Beauty and the Beast* led to more roles in musical theater. In 1998, Jackman won a star-

Jackman shows the ferocity and physicality of Wolverine.

ring role with the London National Theater in England, playing Curly in the musical *Oklahoma!* Jackman has said that being in *Oklahoma!* ranks among his all-time favorite performances. "I totally felt like it can't get any better than this. On some level that production will be one of the highlights of my career." He also had admitted that his success in musicals was completely unexpected. "Musical theater was something of a pleasant surprise for me. There was a musical theater school where I studied acting and I never took those classes."

After *Oklahoma!* Jackman decided to leave musical theater and focus on movie roles. He made his movie debut in the late 1990s, appearing in a few Australian films that were praised by critics but did not do well with audiences. None of them became a hit in the U.S.

Breakout Success: *X-Men*

Jackman's big break came when he was offered a part in the ensemble cast of *X-Men,* released in 2000. In *X-Men,* he was cast as Logan / Wolverine, a mutant superhero with unbreakable bones, the power to heal wounds quickly, and trademark razor-sharp metal claws. Wolverine was his breakout success, his biggest and perhaps best-known movie role—and it almost never happened.

When Jackman first auditioned for the part of Wolverine, he had never read any comic books. He had no idea that the *X-Men* comics were so successful or that the *X-Men* series ranked as one of the best-selling comics of all time. When another actor was cast as Wolverine, Jackman moved on to other projects. But then the original actor had to withdraw from the movie, and Jackman was offered the role. At first, he was going to turn it down. He wasn't sure he wanted to do a comic book movie after all. But something about the character of Wolverine had already left an impression on him. "I think we all feel like mutants and outsiders at some point. That's when I realized that this wasn't your average comic book.

"

"I think we all feel like mutants and outsiders at some point. That's when I realized that this wasn't your average comic book. There was a reason it meant so much to the fans," Jackman acknowledged. "I didn't realize the extent of it, how big a thing it was. But now I meet people with full-color Wolverine tattoos on their backs.... It's the kind of challenge you relish as an actor."

"

A scene from X-Men:
Wolverine with Cyclops, Professor Xavier, Storm, and Jean Grey.

There was a reason it meant so much to the fans," Jackman said. "I didn't realize the extent of it, how big a thing it was. But now I meet people with full-color Wolverine tattoos on their backs.... It's the kind of challenge you relish as an actor; it's there whenever you step into any role that's well-known—Curly in *Oklahoma!*, or Hamlet."

The story of *X-Men* revolves around a group of mutant superheroes, each with a unique superpower that sets them apart from the human world they have sworn to protect. But the human world fears and hates mutants, and it seems that a war between humans and mutants is inevitable. Magneto, an evil mutant, has a plan to prevent this war by turning all humans into mutants. Led by Professor Charles Xavier, the X-Men must act together to stop Magneto before he destroys the human race.

Playing Wolverine

Bringing Wolverine to life turned out to be more challenging than Jackman originally thought. Wolverine had very little dialogue in the movie, but there was still a lot of emotion to convey. To figure out how to do that, Jackman watched Clint Eastwood in the *Dirty Harry* movies and Mel Gibson in *Road Warrior*. "Here were guys who had relatively little dialogue, like Wolverine had, but you knew and felt everything. I'm not normally one to copy, but I wanted to see how these guys achieved it." Meanwhile, the movie's director encouraged Jackman to make Wolverine appear angrier and meaner. Jackman decided to look further into the animal side of the character. "The battle between animal and human, I broke that down to be the most essential thing to focus on with this character," he explained. "We can all relate to that. Maybe not in the extreme level, but we wrestle every day with that argument between chaos and control and freedom and discipline."

Playing Wolverine was also a physically demanding role. Jackman insisted on performing some of his own stunts and worked hard to make Wolverine's fighting style seem realistic. "We worked a lot on the movement style of Wolverine, and I studied some martial arts. I watched a lot of Mike Tyson fights, especially his early fights. There's something about his style, the animal rage, that seemed right for Wolverine," Jackman recalled. "I kept saying to the writers, 'Don't give me long, choreographed fights for the sake of it. Don't make the fights pretty.'" And then there was the issue of Wolverine's lethal claws, which Jackman had to get used to wearing as naturally as Wolverine does. "Every day in my living room, I'd just walk around with those claws, to get used to them. I've got scars on one leg, punctures straight through the cheek, on my forehead. I'm a bit clumsy. I'm lucky I didn't tell them that when I auditioned."

Once the movie was released, Jackman was anxious to know what fans of the *X-Men* comics would think of his portrayal of Wolverine. Two days after the movie opened, Jackman went to a Manhattan movie theater to see the audience reactions for himself. When he got to the theater, he was surprised at the number of people waiting for the next showing of *X-Men*. "There was a huge queue [line] going around the corner. I'm thinking, 'I either have to go to the front and say who I am, but that's not really me, or wait at the end, but those people weren't going to get in anyway.' So I failed."

But Jackman didn't have to wait very long to find out what people thought of the movie. *X-Men* was a huge success with fans and became one of the biggest blockbuster hit movies of 2000, earning almost $300 million worldwide. A film critic for the *Los Angeles Times* called Jackman the star of the movie, saying that he brought a "necessary level of acting intensity" to the role. *Variety* said that Jackman "perfectly brought the comic-book character of Wolverine, a conflicted anti-hero, to vivid life, pleasing general moviegoers and hard core fans of the comic book." Jackman won a Saturn Award from the Academy of Science Fiction, Fantasy & Horror Films, and was nominated for two MTV Movie Awards and a Blockbuster Entertainment Award.

A scene from X2: X-Men United, *with (from left) Iceman, Wolverine, Pyro, and Rogue.*

X2: X-Men United

After the runaway success of *X-Men,* Jackman went on to other projects. Then in 2003, he revived the character of Wolverine for the sequel *X2: X-Men United.* In *X2,* the story picks up just a few months after the events of *X-Men.* There's an assassination attempt on the U.S. president, and that sets off a war between humans and mutants. The X-Men team up with their former arch-enemy, Magneto, to try and stop the elimination of Earth's mutant population.

For Jackman, getting ready for the movie was a lot of work. Returning to the role of Wolverine required him to bulk up physically and to follow a strict weight-lifting routine. He also had to follow a low-fat, high-protein diet in order to gain enough weight. Jackman needed to weigh about 200 pounds for the role, and he struggled to reach that goal. His regimen demanded that he eat special meals every three hours, including waking up in the middle of night just to eat. Every day at four o'clock in the morning, Jackman would get out of bed to eat meals like egg whites and dry toast, or a whole chicken. Then he would go back to bed until it was time to go to the gym.

X2: X-Men United was a lot of fun, with the same types of humor and action sequences that made the first film so popular. But it also dealt with issues of identity, tolerance, and accepting those who are different. Stan Lee, who created the first *X-Men* comic book, has said that he wrote it during the civil rights movement. "I wanted to show the evils of bigotry," Lee once said. These more serious elements reverberated with Jackman also, who was attracted to the sequel so he could explore Wolverine's inner life. "There was one bit of the script where we flash back to Wolverine's origins, the experiments where they turn him into a killing machine. We see Wolverine come out of this laboratory, his body is in absolute agony, he's got blood all over him, he's just killed (his captors), he's got all these knives (coming out of his hands) but he doesn't know who he is, doesn't know anything except this horrific thing happened," he explained. "In that moment, he unleashes that sort of primal scream that you see on the screen and I thought, this is what has burned inside of Wolverine for 15 years. I wanted to make that moment as intense as possible because I felt, it's one of those crisis points in life where you either fold, or you're driven forward."

X2: X-Men United proved to be a huge hit with critics and fans alike, many of whom called it superior to the original film. *Entertainment Weekly* called it "a fun thrill ride that heroically surpasses the original." That view was echoed in the *Seattle Post-Intelligencer.* "On a purely visceral level, the movie is a doozy. Its action sequences and possibly thousands of special effects shots are all seamlessly choreographed to be an exhilarating thrill ride and total immersion in a comic-bookish future/gothic world. The cast of mutant characters with their various shape-shifting, telepathic, telekinetic, teleporting, pyromaniacal and other powers are great fun, and are portrayed with enough flashes of vulnerability and psychological depth to emerge as recognizably human characters." The film ultimately earned over $400 million worldwide at the box office.

"The battle between animal and human, I broke that down to be the most essential thing to focus on with this character," Jackman mused. "We can all relate to that. Maybe not in the extreme level, but we wrestle every day with that argument between chaos and control and freedom and discipline."

X-Men: The Last Stand

Jackman returned to the role of Woverine for the third time in *X-Men: The Last Stand,* released in 2006. In this installment of the *X-Men* series, the

Wolverine and Storm make an amazing discovery in X-Men: The Last Stand*—Jean Grey, who they thought had died.*

war still rages between humans and mutants. Scientists have discovered a cure for mutation, which would permanently turn mutants into humans, taking away their powers and making them "normal." The mutant community becomes divided between those who want the cure and those fighting against it. Many of the mutants struggle with whether it is more important to fit in or to remain an individual. Others are more sure about themselves. "There's nothing to cure," declared the mutant Storm. "There's nothing wrong with any of us." Although the X-Men feel they are hated by the human world, they still believe mutants and humans should be able to live together in an integrated society. But the evil Magneto joins with former allies of the X-Men to build an army to fight the humans and destroy the cure. That leads to a battle between the mutants led by the evil Magneto and those led by the more idealistic Professor X, as the X-Men realize that to end the human-mutant war once and for all, they must once again stop Magneto from destroying humanity.

In *The Last Stand,* as in the earlier *X-Men* movies, many reviewers saw more than just the typical popcorn action flick. Many considered it an allegory on different social issues, viewing the anti-mutant discrimination as racism, anti-Semitism, homophobia, and other forms of hatred against others. For Jackman, though, the characters were the key element. "I wouldn't have gone back to do it if I didn't really like playing the role," he acknowledged. "Wolverine is a bit of a gift as a character because, in all the comic-book movies and action movies, there are not many roles that have this kind of complexity. It is a movie that is really about people. It is about their flaws as much as their abilities and that is what I like about it."

> *"To me, he's one of the great screen archetypes," Jackman declared. "He's like, when I was growing up, Han Solo and Mad Max, or Dirty Harry. These were all the kind of roles I loved. And that's what Wolverine is. He's that reluctant hero. He is a good guy but he's not a nice guy. I think we all love that character. He's the guy you want on your side."*

Still, reviews of the film were divided. While acknowledging that Jackman's performance "again steals the film," *People* complained that the movie was "crowded with so many superpower-endowed mutants … that none of the characters show up long enough to make an impact." But other reviewers were more impressed. "It is action that aspires," wrote the *Globe and Mail.* "Things explode, and explode beautifully. There are deaths, operatic deaths, and the viewer is strangely moved. And at the heart of it is Wolverine, armed with fierce conviction." Reviewers may have been conflicted, but fans clearly were not: they turned out in droves to watch the new installment. The movie earned $120.1 million in its opening weekend alone, making it the largest Memorial Day weekend opening in box-office history and the fourth-largest opening weekend of all time. It went on to earn over $450 million worldwide.

X-Men Origins: Wolverine

After appearing in a string of movies that were not as successful as the *X-Men* series, Jackman revisited the character of Wolverine for the fourth time in 2009 in *X-Men Origins: Wolverine.* This installment of the *X-Men* series capitalized on the popularity of Wolverine. The film serves as a prequel to the previous *X-Men* movies, telling the story of how Logan became the mutant Wolverine. The prologue, opening in 1845, establishes the story of two mutants, Logan (Jackman) and his brother Victor (Sabretooth), and their inhuman strength, agility, and ability to heal their own wounds. The movie goes on to show Logan's relationship with his brother, the beginning of his involvement with William Stryker, the source of his metal

A scene from X-Men Origins: Wolverine, *as he seeks revenge.*

claws, and his struggles between his human and his baser instincts as he seeks revenge.

By focusing on Wolverine's background, Jackman was able to give the character more depth. "Wolverine's fun and cool, but I wouldn't be down for my fourth time doing it if there wasn't something more interesting to it than just slicing and dicing and smoking a cigar and saying a few cool lines." Jackman seemed to have great respect for the character. "To me, he's one of the great screen archetypes. He's like, when I was growing up, Han Solo and Mad Max, or Dirty Harry. These were all the kind of roles I loved. And that's what Wolverine is. He's that reluctant hero. He is a good guy but he's not a nice guy. I think we all love that character. He's the guy you want on your side."

The movie received mixed reviews from critics. "For all its attempts to probe the physiological and psychological roots of its tortured antihero," wrote *Daily Variety,* "this brawny but none-too-brainy prequel sustains the rest mainly—if only fitfully—as a nonstop slice-and-dice vehicle for Hugh Jackman." *USA Today* observed that Jackman "artfully embodies a character who is both ferocious and humane … compelling viewers to care about his metamorphosis." Despite such reviews, fans loved the movie, which earned over $370 million at the box office worldwide. Fans at the 2008

Comic-Con in San Diego, California, went wild when Jackman made a surprise appearance to promote the movie's upcoming release. Jackman earned a Teen Choice Movie Award for his performance.

Branching Out

Between filming movies in the *X-Men* series, Jackman kept busy working on other projects. To avoid being typecast in any one kind of role, he chose a variety of different parts in movies and on stage. From 2001 to 2008, Jackman had roles in serious dramas, romantic comedies, suspense thrillers, and musical theater, and he also did voice acting for animated movies. All of these different projects expanded his fan base and helped to draw new audiences to the *X-Men* movie series.

> *In the future, Jackman hopes to be able to play Wolverine and to perform in stage and movie musicals. "I love both. What I realize now is that I have to have the stage in my professional diet. It's a lot more tiring, particularly doing musicals, but it informs my movie-acting," Jackman said. "In the end, it's all about variety—mixing an action film with something lighter."*

After the first *X-Men* movie, Jackman starred in the 2001 romantic comedy *Kate & Leopold,* playing the role of a time-travelling 19th-century gentleman. For this performance, he was nominated for two awards: the Golden Globe Award for best actor in a comedy or musical and the Hollywood Foreign Press Association Award for best performance by an actor in a motion picture musical or comedy. Then after making *X2,* Jackman returned to musical theater. He starred in the 2003 Broadway production of *The Boy from Oz,* the story of Peter Allen, a flamboyant Australian songwriter who died of AIDS-related cancer in 1992. Jackman won a Tony Award for best actor in a musical for his performance in that play. Jackman then appeared in the movie *Van Helsing,* released in 2004. He starred in the title role as the hero out to kill Dracula, the Wolf Man, and Frankenstein. *Van Helsing* was not a success at the box office or with critics. *People* called the movie "pretty darn dumb, with even the main characters so thinly drawn that one remains indifferent to their fates."

While working on *X-Men: The Last Stand,* Jackman was also providing character voices in two popular animated movies released in 2006. In *Happy Feet,* Jackman was the voice of Memphis, a member of a community of singing

Leaving Wolverine far behind, Jackman did voice work on two animated movies, Happy Feet *(top) and* Flushed Away *(bottom).*

penguins. Memphis's son Mumble cannot sing, but knows how to tap dance instead. The story unfolds as Mumble struggles with being different and ultimately teaches the penguin community that everyone doesn't have to be exactly the same. In *Flushed Away,* Jackman was the voice of Roddy, a cultured high-society rat who lands in the sewers of London after being flushed down the toilet. Roddy learns about the underground world of "real" rats as he undertakes an adventurous journey to get back home. "Roddy fancies himself as a James Bond character. See, I get to live out my fantasies through this movie," Jackman said. "I can see some of my facial expressions, and I can see some of my gestures and things like that because they filmed me in the studio the entire time." Jackman enjoyed voice acting and also appreciated the opportunity to play lighter roles in a family-oriented feature. "It is great to finally have something that my kids can see," he remarked.

Jackman's next big project after *X-Men: The Last Stand* was the World War II-era Western drama *Australia,* released in 2008. Jackman starred opposite Nicole Kidman in the role of the nameless Drover (cowboy) hired to drive a herd of cattle across the inhospitable Australian outback. "This is definitely the straight-down-the-line, classic, old-school leading-man role I've been waiting for," he remarked. To prepare for the role, he trained in horseback riding and wrangling cattle like a real cowboy. One scene of the film required Jackman to lasso a wild horse. His characteristic dedication and intensive practice helped him do it. "The horse went ballistic when I got that rope around his neck," he admitted. "My gloves ripped, the rope peeled skin off my hands. I just remember being so happy that I did it that I didn't care at all." Unfortunately, *Australia* was not well-received by critics, who generally dismissed it as unoriginal and clichéd. However, the *New York Times* credited Jackman's performance with giving the film "oomph." *Newsweek* called Jackman "gruff and hunky," while *USA Today* praised his performance as the "rough-hewn cattle driver."

Future Plans

Recognizing that *X-Men* gave him his big break as an actor, Jackman hopes to be able to play Wolverine in more films in the future. He is also interested in continuing to perform in stage productions and in movie versions of musicals. "I love both. What I realize now is that I have to have the stage in my professional diet. It's a lot more tiring, particularly doing musicals, but it informs my movie-acting," Jackman said. "In the end, it's all about variety—mixing an action film with something lighter."

Part of the appeal of such a diverse performing career is the variety of opportunities for reaching different audiences. Action movies and Broadway musicals seem to be on nearly opposite ends of the performing arts spectrum, but Jackman enjoys mixing up his roles to keep his performances fresh. "I'm the same as everyone else in the audience. I get sick of seeing the same faces after a while and I know that this amazing run of roles I've been getting will one day just grind to a halt and nobody will want to know me for ages." But for now, Jackman's popularity shows no sign of waning.

Jackman has often been compared to such other well-known Australian actors as Mel Gibson, Russell Crowe, and Heath Ledger. Jackman doesn't mind the comparisons, saying, "I watched Mel in all those *Road Warrior* movies and he was just brilliant. I thought if I could just be half as good." In fact, Jackman credits his versatility as a performer to his Australian roots. He believes that the relative isolation of the island continent requires people to develop diverse talents. "With a population of just 20 million, you can't be too fussy. You have to be able to do everything. That may be some of the reason Australian actors have done well. There's more versatility to what they can do. Plus, we have a saying here: Have a go. We don't like people who play things safe. It's not enough just to be successful. You have to take a bit of a risk," Jackman said. "Greater than my fear of failure—which we all have—is my fear of mediocrity and of being hemmed in by just the lack of courage to try something.... The worst thing is not to have a go."

MARRIAGE AND FAMILY

Jackman married Deborra-Lee Furness in 1996. They have two adopted children, a son, Oscar Maximilian, born in 2000, and a daughter, Ava Eliot, born in 2005.

HOBBIES AND OTHER INTERESTS

In his spare time, Jackman enjoys dancing, windsurfing, playing piano and guitar, and practicing yoga and meditation. He can juggle five balls at once, and he knows the score of every Rodgers and Hammerstein musical by heart. Whenever Jackman is shooting a movie, every Friday he brings a bag of lottery tickets to the set. He gives tickets to everyone working on the movie. "You know, ever since I started 'Lucky Friday,' I never get a Friday off," he joked. "I think people are hooked on those lottery tickets."

SELECTED CREDITS

"Correlli," 1995 (TV series)
Beauty and the Beast, 1996 (musical theater)
Sunset Boulevard, 1997 (musical theater)
Oklahoma!, 1998 (musical theater)

Erskinville Kings, 1999 (movie)
Paperback Hero, 1999 (movie)
X-Men, 2000 (movie)
Kate & Leopold, 2001 (movie)
Someone Like You, 2001 (movie)
The Boy from Oz, 2003 (musical theater)
X2: X-Men United, 2003 (movie)
Van Helsing, 2004 (movie)
The Fountain, 2006 (movie)
The Prestige, 2006 (movie)
Flushed Away, 2006 (movie)
Happy Feet, 2006 (movie)
X-Men: The Last Stand, 2006 (movie)
Australia, 2008 (movie)
X-Men Origins: Wolverine, 2009 (movie)
"A Steady Rain," 2009 (play)

HONORS AND AWARDS

Variety Club Award: 1998, for *Oklahoma!*
Saturn Award (Academy of Science Fiction, Fantasy & Horror Films): 2000, for *X-Men*
Tony Award: 2004, Best Actor in a Musical, for *The Boy from Oz*
Emmy Award: 2005, Outstanding Individual Performance in a Variety or Music Program, for hosting the 58th Annual Tony Awards
Teen Choice Movie Award: 2008, Choice Movie Actor in an Action Adventure, for *X-Men Origins: Wolverine*

FURTHER READING

Periodicals

Biography, May 2003, p.46
Current Biography Yearbook, 2003
Entertainment Weekly, Aug. 22, 2008; Apr. 24, 2009, p.26
Globe & Mail (Toronto, Canada), May 27, 2006, p.R14
Interview, Sep. 2003, p.171; May 2004, p.99; June 2006, p.38
Newsweek, May 18, 2009, p.67
New York Times, July 21, 2000, p.E18; Sep. 7, 2008, p.36
O, The Oprah Magazine, June 2006, p.242
People, Aug. 7, 2000, p. 81; May 14, 2001, p.95; May 24, 2004, p.24
Time, Oct. 20, 2003, p.72
USA Today, Oct. 17, 2007, p.D12; Apr. 27, 2009, p.D1

Online Articles

http://www.allmovie.com
(AllMovie, "Hugh Jackman Biography," 2009)
http://www.variety.com
(Variety, "Hugh Jackman: Biography," 2009)

ADDRESS

Hugh Jackman
The Endeavor Agency
9601 Wilshire Blvd., 3rd Floor
Beverly Hills, CA 90210

WORLD WIDE WEB SITES

http://marvel.com/movies/X-Men.X-Men_~op~2000~ep~
http://marvel.com/movies/X-Men.X2~colon~_X-Men_United
http://marvel.com/movies/X-Men.X3~colon~_The_Last_Stand
http://marvel.com/movies/X-Men.X-Men_Origins~colon~_Wolverine
http://marvel.com/universe/X-Men

Christianne Meneses Jacobs 1971-

Nicaraguan-Born American Writer and Teacher
Creator of Spanish-Language Children's Magazines *Iguana* and *¡Yo Sé!*

BIRTH

Christianne Meneses Jacobs was born Christianne Marcelle Meneses Palma on March 28, 1971, in Managua, Nicaragua, a country in Central America located just north of the equator. In Nicaragua, her father, Enrique Meneses Peña, was a lawyer and politician, while her mother, Thelma A. Meneses, worked as a legal secretary. After moving to the United States, both of her parents had jobs checking luggage at the Los Angeles International Airport. She has one younger brother, Enrique M. Meneses.

YOUTH AND EDUCATION

As a young girl growing up in Nicaragua, Meneses Jacobs enjoyed a comfortable life. Her grandfather, Dr. Ildefonso Palma Martinez, was a highly respected lawyer, law professor, and a justice on the Nicaraguan Supreme Court. Her father was a lawyer and the vice-president of the National Liberal Party, which at that time was one of Nicaragua's large political organizations. Meneses Jacobs has described her childhood years as privileged. "I attended private school and ballet lessons. We had domestic servants that performed several jobs: nannies, cook, chauffer, gardener, cleaning, laundry, and ironing." Her whole family, including aunts, uncles, and cousins, took vacations together at the beach, swimming and collecting shells. Iguanas (large tropical lizards) lived in her backyard, and every day around noon they came out to bathe in the hot sun.

"Meneses Jacobs has described her childhood years as privileged. "I attended private school and ballet lessons. We had domestic servants that performed several jobs: nannies, cook, chauffer, gardener, cleaning, laundry, and ironing.""

But Meneses Jacobs's childhood experiences were also closely tied to the political situation in Nicaragua during that time. After years of economic instability and accusations of government corruption, civil war broke out in the late 1970s. Meneses Jacobs recalled, "The Sandinista revolution occurred when I was eight years old. I remember the civil war and the attacks on the small towns." The Sandinista National Liberation Front, known as the Sandinistas, fought against the existing government for control of Nicaragua. Fighting quickly spread to towns and cities throughout the country, and many people died.

The existing government was eventually overthrown by the Sandinistas, but this did not end the war. Some Nicaraguans did not support the Sandinistas and thought they should not be allowed to run the government. An opposing army known as the Contras (short for "Contrarrevolución Nacional," meaning National Counter-Revolution) fought against the Sandinistas. The Contras were supported by some of the former Nicaraguan leaders, who fled Nicaragua when the Sandinistas took over the government.

The Contras were also supported by the U.S. government, which opposed the Sandinistas, partly because of their ties to Communist countries like Cuba. All of this created a complicated political situation involving many countries in Central America, Europe, and the Middle East. During this time, life for many Nicaraguans was dangerous and difficult. Fighting was still going on, and widespread food shortages affected everyone.

Leaving Nicaragua

Trouble soon came to Meneses Jacobs's father and their family, in part because he worked as an attorney. "My father was on the defense team for an American pilot whose plane was shot down by the Sandinista artillery at the border of Nicaragua and Costa Rica in December of 1997," she stated. "The American pilot was accused of being a CIA agent." At this time, the Sandinistas suspected the U.S. Central Intelligence Agency (CIA) of spying in order to help the Contras. It was very dangerous for Meneses Jacobs's father to defend the American pilot, but he did. The pilot was eventually freed by the Sandinistas and allowed to return to the U.S. By then, it was no longer safe for Meneses Jacobs's family to stay in Nicaragua. "Three months later we left Nicaragua," she recalled. "The Sandinista government had threatened my father's life and he realized that the country was unsafe. I left March 19, 1988. My parents and brother arrived a week later in Los Angeles."

Meneses Jacobs was 17 years old when she and her family relocated to Los Angeles. When they left Nicaragua, the family was allowed to take only $500 with them. "One day you are rich and you are affluent … and you have maids, cooks, a driver, and nannies," she remembered. "And the next day, you come to this country and you are poor and you have nothing." Although in Nicaragua her parents were highly educated professionals with careers, in the United States they could only find work checking luggage at the Los Angeles International Airport. "It was pretty hard for them to support me and my brother on less than $20,000 a year," Meneses Jacobs said. Looking back on that time, she realized that the sacrifices her parents made then allowed her and her brother "[to] finally enjoy the opportunities of freedom [and] taught us to speak up when there is injustice."

Adjusting to Life in the U.S.

Life in the U.S. turned out to be very different from life in Nicaragua. One of the first differences that struck Meneses Jacobs was the abundance of food and the attitude of most Americans. "I was particularly surprised (and continue to be surprised) by the amount of food that is wasted in this country," she observed. "We had a food rationing card in Nicaragua and

Meneses Jacobs with her magazine's namesake.

had to pick up one pound of rice, one pound of beans, one pound of sugar, and one quart of oil per person in the household for a two-week period."

Language was another big difference. When she first arrived in the U.S., Meneses Jacobs had trouble with English. This made going to Los Angeles High School difficult. "The most challenging part was that I was a senior in high school in Nicaragua but I was placed in the 10th grade at L.A. High because I did not speak English well," she revealed. "It was also challenging that although I had studied English in Nicaragua I could not understand it in the U.S. That lasted for my first four months and was very frustrating." Meneses Jacobs refused to allow the language barrier to become a permanent setback. She worked hard to improve her English and quickly overcame that challenge. She credits her high school teachers for helping her succeed. "They encouraged me every day to rise above expectations. I will always be grateful to them for I would not be who I am now without their nurturing and encouragement."

While in high school, Meneses Jacobs was also inspired by local television news anchor Carla Aragon. "One of my role models was anchorwoman Carla Aragon (who is now in Albuquerque). I met her in high school and established a friendship with her for several years while we lived in L.A. She once called me 'a diamond in the rough waiting to be discovered.' She was my role model for an educated, professional, and successful Latina."

Meneses Jacobs was a serious student who excelled in all of her classes and became the Editor-in-Chief of both the Spanish and English school newspapers. "I adapted to the American school system fairly quickly," she recalled. "At the beginning, I thought it was so strange that we all had to move classrooms and run to different floors of the school building. I was very confused. In Nicaragua, the teachers rotate and the students stay in the same classroom."

Meneses Jacobs faced many challenges adjusting to her new life, but she also said, "I am glad I moved when I was 17 years old. I had a strong educational foundation and a sense of who I was. As a result, I was not an easy target for peer pressure." There were also some things she liked about life in the U.S. "As I began to understand the American way of life, I began to like the idea of meritocracy [a system in which individuals are rewarded for their achievements]. I admired Americans that worked hard and became successful in their careers. I believe that one's dreams are possible when one has the motivation and willingness to work hard."

"One day you are rich and you are affluent ... and you have maids, cooks, a driver, and nannies," Meneses Jacobs said about her experience before and after her family immigrated to the U.S. "And the next day, you come to this country and you are poor and you have nothing."

Meneses Jacobs graduated from Los Angeles High School when she was 20 years old. She received a scholarship to attend Wesleyan University in Middletown, Connecticut. At Wesleyan, Meneses Jacobs studied government and international relations. She earned a Bachelor's Degree from Wesleyan in 1995. She later went on to earn a Master's Degree in education in 2001 and a Reading Specialist Certification in 2005.

CAREER HIGHLIGHTS

Meneses Jacobs originally planned a career in the entertainment industry, working with Latino filmmakers. But by the time she graduated college in 1995, she realized that teaching children would be a better choice for her. She had returned to Los Angeles after graduation, and a friend mentioned that the public school system was looking for bilingual teachers. Meneses Jacobs called to find out about possible job openings, and was asked if she could come in right away. She began teaching second grade that same day.

Supporting Bilingualism

In 1998, Meneses Jacobs was married to Marc Jacobs who was not a native Spanish speaker. They had their first daughter in 2001. Before their daughter was born, they had already decided to raise their children in a bilingual (two language) family. They strongly believed in the importance of exposing their children to the Spanish language and Latin American heritage. When their daughter was born, they decided that Meneses Jacobs would speak only Spanish at home and her husband would speak only English. In this way, they hoped their daughter would naturally learn both languages.

"My advice to bilingual children is to continue learning more about their chosen language," Meneses Jacobs said. "We are living in a global economy and parents need to help their children understand that being bilingual, or multilingual, is an asset to them. Being bilingual in this country is a necessity, not just a cultural pride. Anyone who wants to be successful needs to learn a second language."

This worked well except in the case of reading together, or finding books to begin teaching their daughter to read. Almost everything was in English. The Spanish books that were available for children were poorly translated versions of English books. "When my oldest daughter was two she became more interested in words and books," Meneses Jacobs explained. "As a teacher, I knew that it was important to expose her to Spanish through reading. I searched for books and magazines in Spanish that were not translations of English-language works. However, I discovered that it was difficult to find quality literature written in Spanish."

When she couldn't find the books that she wanted for her daughter, Meneses Jacobs started thinking about creating a new source of Spanish-language stories for children. She thought that a magazine could provide a mix of entertaining and educational stories that would be interesting to children and their parents. "My husband and I realized that a magazine could deliver a variety of original Spanish-language materials for parents. We researched the idea for over a year." As her idea began to take shape, Meneses Jacobs had the complete support of her husband. "He believed in my idea from the very beginning and has not stopped supporting and en-

The Spanish-language magazine Iguana *contains fiction, biographies, and fun activities for kids.*

couraging me," Meneses Jacobs said. "My husband and I initially used our own savings and personally financed the launch of the magazine."

Iguana

In 2005, Meneses Jacobs published the first issue of her new magazine, *Iguana*. It is the first Spanish-language magazine created especially for readers aged seven to 12. The magazine's goal is to encourage young people to be proud of their native language and culture. As she remarked, "I want kids to learn about our people, take ownership about who they are and what they can aspire to be." Meneses Jacobs is the editor, and her husband is the art director. They create *Iguana* with contributions from Spanish-speaking writers around the world. Each issue includes fictional stories, biographies, interviews with people who have influenced the lives of Latinos in America, true stories about children around the world, recipes, crafts, puzzles, and artwork and poetry from readers.

As the first publication of its kind, *Iguana* received a tremendously positive response. The magazine has been universally praised by experts in children's literature, who have called it "snappy," "readable," and "lighthearted." As Meneses Jacobs pointed out, "We have received a very enthusiastic response from teachers, especially those in bilingual and dual-language schools. Parents are delighted that they can pick up the magazine and read to and with their children. Librarians are the most enthusiastic because they see its educational value and they can offer an alternative for their Hispanic patrons." The education community recognized *Iguana*'s importance with the 2009 Multicultural Children's Publication Award from the National Association for Multicultural Education.

In addition, the magazine has been welcomed by Spanish speakers in the U.S. and abroad. After placing an Internet advertisement to find contributing writers, Meneses Jacobs was overwhelmed by responses from Venezuela, Mexico, Argentina, Puerto Rico and the U.S. *Iguana* has also been a hit with non-native speakers of Spanish. "It surprised us to learn that many Anglo families are discovering *Iguana* and subscribing for their children who attend Spanish-immersion schools or dual-language programs. We also receive many subscriptions from adults who are learning Spanish."

¡Yo Sé!

The success of *Iguana* inspired Meneses Jacobs to create a second Spanish-language publication for young people. *¡Yo Sé!* (meaning "I know!") was launched in 2009 as a kids' page in more than 40 different Spanish-language newspapers. Each *¡Yo Sé!* page includes short articles about popular culture, celebrities, upcoming movies and television shows, biographies, interviews with Latino personalities, features on young Latinos who are making a difference in the world, comics, and more. Meneses Jacobs created *¡Yo Sé!* to help parents and children preserve the Spanish language together. "This is my literacy campaign. I'm on a quest to teach Latino parents they have to read to their children every night." In the future, Meneses Jacobs hopes to expand *¡Yo Sé!* into a small magazine that can be included as a weekly newspaper insert.

Meneses Jacobs firmly believes in the importance of bilingualism, particularly in Spanish. "The Hispanic community continues to grow at a high rate," she asserted. "As the population grows in importance so does the Spanish language. Because of that growth, the Spanish language has positioned itself as the second language of this country. The Spanish language will continue to grow and will not die because millions of immigrants will continue to keep it alive." She especially believes in the importance of bilingualism in the schools. "It is a shame that many individuals are so narrow minded that they help pass legislation against the use of any language other than English. It is a shame that many Hispanic children are not given the opportunity to learn their own language because of the elimination of bilingual education programs. I have seen the rise of dual language programs at public schools that are offered to non-Spanish speaking children. The opportunity for Hispanic children to participate in this kind of programs is taken away from them. As a result, many Hispanic children are growing up not knowing how to read or write in their own language. By taking their language away, the school system is robbing these children of their culture and heritage."

> *"Believe in yourself. There are days when the overwhelming amount of work, the rejections,... and the constant pressures of life, can make quitting seem attractive, but you have to persevere. This is your dream and you can make it happen. You have to believe in yourself—and work really hard, too."*

Meneses Jacobs hopes that resources like *Iguana* and *¡Yo Sé!* will help preserve the Spanish language and Latino cultures while preparing young people for their futures in a changing world. "My advice to bilingual children is to continue learning more about their chosen language," she said. "Learning to speak the language is not enough, children must learn to read and write like native speakers. We are living in a global economy and parents need to help their children understand that being bilingual, or multilingual, is an asset to them. Being bilingual in this country is a necessity, not just a cultural pride. Anyone who wants to be successful needs to learn a second language."

Meneses Jacobs after winning the Anna Maria Arias Memorial Business Fund Award, recognized for her innovation, achievement, and community service.

Future Plans

Meneses Jacobs still works as a teacher and plans to continue publishing *Iguana*. Eventually, she would like *Iguana* to be distributed internationally, to reach Spanish-speaking children everywhere. For now, though, cost is the biggest obstacle in the way of that goal. "The biggest challenge was to find funding," she acknowledged. "My husband and I started *Iguana* by using our personal savings. *Iguana* is an educational magazine. Therefore, it does not contain advertising. The magazine sustains itself with subscriptions. It has also been a challenge to market and distribute the magazine due to a limited budget."

Meneses Jacobs is committed to meeting any challenges that the future may hold. "Life's journey is like an obstacle course," she observed. "Our job is to reach the finish line with our dreams intact. Some of those obstacles might be hard to overcome but the key is to never lose sight of the dream. We must achieve that dream with perseverance. All is lost if we give up. We will live a frustrated life if we don't try to overcome those obstacles." For Meneses Jacobs, perseverance, hard work, and belief in self are the tools to succeed. "Believe in yourself. There are days when the overwhelming amount of work, the rejections,… and the constant pressures of life, can make quitting seem attractive, but you have to persevere. This is your dream and you can make it happen. You have to believe in yourself—and work really hard, too."

MARRIAGE AND FAMILY

Meneses Jacobs married Marc Jacobs, a graphic artist, in October 1998. They live in Scottsdale, Arizona, and have two daughters, Isabelle Selene (born in 2001) and Katherine Celeste (born in 2005).

Meneses Jacobs was raised Catholic but converted to Judaism after graduating college. "When I met my (future) husband, Marc Jacobs, I asked if he was Jewish, but I didn't tell him I was studying Judaism," she revealed.

"After graduation, I moved back to Los Angeles and studied with a rabbi for three more years. In March 1998, I converted. It was very emotional. I felt I was detaching from my parents, but my father gave me a big hug and said in Spanish, 'God of any religion is a good God.' In May of that year, my husband proposed, and we got married in October."

HONORS AND AWARDS

Anna Maria Arias Memorial Business Fund Award (*Latina Style* magazine): 2007

Multicultural Children's Publication Award (National Association for Multicultural Education): 2009, for *Iguana*

FURTHER READING

Periodicals

Arizona Republic, Apr. 18, 2005, p.D5; Sep. 27, 2007
Criticas, June 15, 2008
Jewish News of Greater Phoenix, Spring 2008, p.8
NEA Today, Apr. 2006

Online Articles

http://www.criticasmagazine.com/article/ca6560349.html
(Criticas, "Spanish-Speaking Iguana Turns Three," June 15, 2008)
http://www.latinopm.com
(Latino Perspectives, "A Happy Niche," June 2006)

ADDRESS

Christianne Meneses Jacobs
Iguana Magazine
NicaGal, LLC
PO Box 26432
Scottsdale AZ 85255

WORLD WIDE WEB SITES

http://www.iguanamagazine.com
http://www.nicagal.com

Alexander Ovechkin 1985-

Russian Professional Hockey Player with the Washington Capitals
Winner of the Hart Trophy as the NHL's Most Valuable Player in 2008 and 2009

BIRTH

Alexander Ovechkin, known as Alex or Ovi to his friends, was born on September 17, 1985, in Moscow, Russia. At that time, Russia was part of the Union of Soviet Socialist Republics (USSR), or the Soviet Union. His mother, Tatiana Nikolaevna Ovechkina, was one of Russia's greatest female basketball players. She won Olympic gold medals in 1976 and 1980 as

Ovechkin (center) after leading the Russian team to the gold medal at the 2003 World Junior Hockey Championships.

the starting point guard for the Soviet national women's team. After her athletic career ended, she became president of the Dynamo Moscow women's professional basketball team. Alex's father, Mikhail Ovechkin, was a professional soccer player until his career was cut short by a leg injury. He later worked as a taxi driver and as a director for his wife's basketball team. Alex had two older brothers, Sergei and Mikhail. Sadly, Sergei died in a car accident when Alex was 10.

YOUTH

Ovechkin became fascinated with the sport of hockey at a very young age. When he was just two years old, he picked up a hockey stick and helmet in a sporting-goods store and refused to put them down. His interest grew when he saw his first hockey game on television. "When he was about four years old, the first time he saw hockey on TV, his jaw just dropped and he froze," his father remembered. "That was the only thing he wanted to watch." Before long, Ovechkin had started a collection of National Hockey League (NHL) trading cards that eventually totaled around 2,000 cards.

By the time Ovechkin joined a youth hockey league at the age of eight, however, he discovered that some of the other boys had already been skating for several years. Determined to catch up with his peers, Ovechkin worked hard to improve his skills. He woke up early in the morning to practice before school, and he stayed late after team practices. "He would skate there until his legs fell off," his father recalled. "He'd come home every evening just completely exhausted. He would drop in the hallway, and we'd pick him up and just carry him to his room."

"When he was about four years old, the first time he saw hockey on TV, his jaw just dropped and he froze," Ovechkin's father remembered. "That was the only thing he wanted to watch."

Ovechkin's hard work paid off, though, as he quickly emerged as one of Russia's top young hockey players. He started playing professionally at the age of 16 for the Dynamo Moscow hockey team in the Russian Superleague. He scored 8 goals and made 8 assists in 40 games as a teenaged rookie playing against much older and more experienced men. Ovechkin played with the Dynamo for the next three seasons as well. By the time he left the team he had scored 36 goals and tallied 32 assists in 152 career games.

Ovechkin also represented Russia in international hockey tournaments throughout his teen years. In 2002 he played for the Russian team at the International Ice Hockey Federation (IIHF) World Under-18 Junior Championships. He led the team to a gold medal by scoring 14 goals in 8 games. The following year he moved up to the World Under-20 Junior Championships. Ovechkin led the tournament with 6 goals to help Russia claim another gold medal. In 2004 he earned a silver medal at the Junior Worlds and also became the youngest player ever to play for the Russian national men's ice hockey team at the IIHF World Championships.

EDUCATION

Ovechkin attended the Military Institute in Moscow during his early hockey career. His studies there fulfilled the mandatory military service requirement that Russia imposed on all of its young male citizens.

CAREER HIGHLIGHTS

NHL—The Washington Capitals

Ovechkin's outstanding performance in the Russian professional league and in international competition brought him to the attention of NHL scouts. Ever since he had started collecting hockey cards as a kid, he had dreamed of playing in the NHL someday. "It's the best hockey there is and I think I'm ready to play there," he declared. "It has always been my dream to play in North America and in the NHL."

As soon as Ovechkin turned 18 and became eligible for the NHL, it became clear that he would be the top player selected in the 2004 entry draft. The Washington Capitals won the first pick in the league's draft lottery because the team had finished 28th out of 30 NHL teams during the previous season (2003-04). "We were all excited," Capitals General Manager George McPhee related. "I called our chief amateur scout. I said, 'If you had to pick today, who would you take?' He said, 'It's got to be Ovechkin.' We just felt like Alex's character and his physical playing really separated him from any other player we could see."

Ovechkin was thrilled to be chosen first overall in the draft, and he expressed great excitement about joining the Capitals. The start of his NHL career was delayed, however, by a labor-management dispute between the NHL Players Association and team owners. They held lengthy negotiations but failed to reach an agreement on several important issues. Since both sides refused to play without a new contract, the entire 2004-05 NHL season was canceled. It marked the first time in the history of American professional sports that a whole season was lost to a labor dispute. The situation, which became known as the NHL lockout, made many hockey fans angry. They felt that greed and selfishness had overtaken the sport.

Ovechkin returned to Dynamo Moscow during the NHL lockout. "There are still things that I can work on with the Dynamo," he explained. "I'd rather be playing there than not playing at all. I always want to be playing hockey. It's what I love. Hockey, hockey, hockey." When the NHL team owners and players' union finally reached an agreement in July 2005, Ovechkin immediately signed a contract with the Capitals and joined the team in Washington DC.

Making Waves as NHL Rookie of the Year

Ovechkin made his NHL debut on October 5, 2005, and immediately established himself as one of the most promising young players in the league. Wearing jersey number 8, which had been his mother's number

Ovechkin celebrates after scoring his first goal in the second period of his first game in the NHL, 2005.

when she played basketball in the Olympics, the young left wing scored two goals in his first NHL game to lead his team to a 3-2 victory over the Columbus Blue Jackets. He went on to score a point in each of his first seven games (in hockey, a player receives a point for scoring a goal or assisting on a goal by a teammate). "He has exceeded expectations," McPhee acknowledged. "We were hoping that he would just hold down a regular shift and contribute in his first year."

As the season progressed, Ovechkin impressed hockey fans with his unique combination of speed, scoring ability, physical play, and obvious enthusiasm for the game. He also made a number of amazing plays that showed up on TV sports highlight reels and Internet video sites. One memorable example came on January 16, 2006, during the third period of a game against the Phoenix Coyotes. Ovechkin sped toward the Coyotes' goal and got knocked off his feet as he prepared to fire a backhand shot. While sliding on his back across the ice, he somehow managed to extend his stick over his head and knock the puck into the goal. "We all lost our minds on the bench," recalled Capitals goalie Ollie Kolzig. "A talent like his only comes along once in a lifetime."

In February 2006 the NHL suspended play for two weeks to allow its best skaters to play in the Winter Olympic Games in Turin, Italy. Ovechkin led

> *"We were all excited," Washington Capitals General Manager George McPhee said when they drafted Ovechkin. "I called our chief amateur scout. I said, 'If you had to pick today, who would you take?' He said, 'It's got to be Ovechkin.' We just felt like Alex's character and his physical playing really separated him from any other player we could see."*

the Russian national team with five goals and was named to the all-tournament team. Although Russia finished fourth and failed to win a medal, Ovechkin enjoyed his Olympic experience. "It was the coolest time in my life to play in the Olympics," he said. "In Russia you know we have a [proud Olympic] history and also my family has a history."

After returning to the Capitals, Ovechkin put the finishing touches on a great rookie season. He set a team record by scoring 52 goals and added 54 assists for a total of 106 points. He thus became the first player in NHL history to register more than 50 goals and 100 points in his rookie season. Ovechkin also became the first rookie to be named to the NHL All-Star Team in 15 years, earned the Kharlamov Trophy as the best Russian player in the league, and easily won the Calder Memorial Trophy as the NHL's Rookie of the Year. Although the Capitals only won 29 games and failed to make the playoffs, Ovechkin felt confident that his team would soon become a contender. "Right now our team is starting out. We will play better and better and better," he predicted. "I look forward to playing many years with the Washington Capitals, and my goal is to win Stanley Cup."

Winning Hearts and the Hart Trophy

Ovechkin's dynamic play continued in the 2006-07 NHL season, during which he tallied 46 goals and 92 points. "He's all over the place," said Capitals captain Chris Clark. "He's not just hitting guys, he's running over guys. If he's not shooting the puck on net, he's driving to the net. He's making something happen on every shift." Ovechkin was voted into the starting lineup for the NHL All-Star Game and received his second consecutive Kharlamov Trophy. Despite his efforts, however, the Capitals only managed to win 28 games and failed to make the playoffs once again. "We have not seen the limits of what Alex can do," said McPhee. "He is one of the most creative players we have seen in a long time. He's only going to

Here Ovechkin shoots the puck past Phidelphia Flyer goalie Martin Biron in Game 6 of the 2008 Eastern Conference playoffs, but the Capitals ultimately lost the playoff series to the Flyers.

improve, and we're going to see how good he can be. If we make the club better, people will see a lot more of him."

As the 2007-08 NHL season got underway, Ovechkin was determined to lead his team into the playoffs. The Capitals struggled early, though, and sat in last place with the worst record in the league at the end of November. Desperate to salvage the season, team management hired a new head coach, Bruce Boudreau. The move had its desired effect. Under Boudreau's guidance, Ovechkin and his teammates improved significantly. In fact, the Capitals made the largest single-season comeback in NHL history. Washington won 11 of the last 12 games on its way to 43 victories and a coveted spot in the playoffs.

The excitement surrounding the young team spread quickly throughout Washington DC and the surrounding area. The Capitals started selling out home games for the first time in franchise history. "Now we bring the fans and the crowd is very good. When it's full, it's unbelievable," Ovechkin stated. "Everybody has to understand, one player cannot bring a good team. It's a whole team. We just have a great team right now, a young team, and everybody does what they can try to do to win."

As in his previous two seasons, Ovechkin remained the undisputed star of the team. He scored a franchise-record 65 goals during the regular season. He thus became the first NHL player in a decade to break 60 goals—and one of only a dozen players ever to score 65 or more. Ovechkin also contributed 47 assists to lead the league in points with 112. His outstanding play continued in the playoffs, where he notched 4 goals and 5 assists, but the Capitals lost a tough seven-game series to the Philadelphia Flyers in the first round.

Ovechkin's remarkable season was recognized with a slew of prestigious postseason awards. He received the Hart Memorial Trophy as the league's most valuable player, the Lester B. Pearson Award for outstanding player as voted by peers, the Maurice Richard Trophy as the NHL's leading goal scorer, and the Art Ross Trophy as the league leader in points. He became the first player ever to capture all four major awards in a single season. "I think I'm the happiest 22-year-old guy on the planet," he said afterward. "I wanted to win everything. Maybe next year the Stanley Cup."

Ovechkin capped off his great year in 2008 by helping the Russian national ice hockey team win a gold medal at the World Championships. He led the team with 6 goals and 6 assists in 9 tournament games. Russia's strong performance made it one of the medal favorites for the 2010 Winter Olympic Games, scheduled to be held in February 2010 in Vancouver, Canada.

A Stellar Season

Prior to the start of the 2008-09 season, Ovechkin signed a 13-year, $124 million contract extension with the Capitals, making him the highest-paid player in NHL history. As the season got underway, Ovechkin proved that management's faith in him was justified. With the young Russian star leading the way, the Capitals competed for the best record in the entire Eastern Conference. "He's playing more of a team game. I think he has a better surrounding cast on the whole, but it's not all about scoring goals. It's about playing to win," Coach Boudreau explained. "There's just nobody that does what Ovechkin does. He shoots the puck harder, crashes into the net. He does what he needs to do to win. He plays hard all the time. We've got a good team, but we'd be nowhere without Alex."

In February 2009 Ovechkin scored his 200th career goal, becoming only the fourth player in league history to accomplish this feat in four NHL seasons. The following month he scored his 50th goal of the season—and one of the most controversial goals of his career—during a game against the Tampa Bay Lightning. He celebrated the goal by dropping his stick on the ice in front of the opposing goaltender, warming his hands over it as if it were on fire, and then pretending that the stick was too hot to pick up. Many people criticized Ovechkin's behavior as unsportsmanlike. Although the NHL does not penalize excessive celebrations, critics claimed that he broke a longstanding tradition by rubbing his goal in the face of his opponents. "To do that, especially on our ice, I took it as an insult," said Lightning wing Ryan Malone. "It's embarrassing. This isn't football."

On the other hand, some people appreciated Ovechkin's showmanship. Supporters found his exuberance entertaining and claimed that he attracted new fans to the sport. They noted, for example, that the Capitals' 2008-09 TV ratings were 65 percent higher than the previous season—and 182 percent higher than they had been during Ovechkin's rookie year.

According to the Washington Capitals head coach, Bruce Boudreau, "There's just nobody that does what Ovechkin does. He shoots the puck harder, crashes into the net. He does what he needs to do to win. He plays hard all the time. We've got a good team, but we'd be nowhere without Alex."

”

Ovechkin finished the regular season with 56 goals and 54 assists for 110 points. He earned a second consecutive Richard Trophy as the league leader in goals scored, and he finished second in points for the season. He also led the NHL with an amazing 528 shots on goal—156 more than any other player. Ovechkin's outstanding performance was honored with a second straight Hart Trophy and Pearson Award as the NHL's most valuable player.

Reaching for a Stanley Cup

Ovechkin and his teammates entered the 2008-09 postseason in a confident mood. After all, the Capitals had won 50 games to claim first place in the Southeast Division of the Eastern Conference. In the first round of the playoffs, Washington defeated the New York Rangers in a tense 7-game series. The Capitals thus advanced to face the Pittsburgh Penguins in the Conference semifinals. The highly anticipated series featured a matchup between Ovechkin and Penguins star Sidney Crosby, who had entered the

Ovechkin faces off against Sidney Crosby of the Pittsburgh Penguins in game 1 of the 2009 conference semifinals, a highly anticipated matchup between the two players that many consider the league's best young players.

league the same year. (For more information on Crosby, see *Biography Today Sports,* Vol. 14.) The young rivals had teamed up in the NHL All-Star Game, but their head-to-head meetings during the season were marked by verbal exchanges and shoving matches. "There's more to stars meeting here, great hockey players meeting, there's great personalities, strong personalities, there's faces of the league that are clashing," said Penguins Coach Dan Bylsma. "That's great for the league, great for the postseason."

In the end, Crosby and the Penguins beat Ovechkin and the Capitals in a hotly contested 7-game series. Ovechkin shone in the playoffs once again, contributing 11 goals and 10 assists for 21 points in 14 games. He hoped that the additional playoff experience would help to prepare his team to reach the Stanley Cup finals in 2009-10. "It's time for us," Ovechkin declared. "The organization, the guys understand that if we make the playoffs, it's not [enough]. Now we have to move forward."

Many hockey analysts believe that Ovechkin, who has been described in the *New York Times* as "the league's best as well as its most exciting and charismatic player," stands ready to lead his team to a championship. Some observers claim that his remarkable skills and pure love of hockey have already changed the face of the game. "If there was ever an athlete who you'd pay to see no matter what his team did, he'd be the guy," said Columbus Blue Jackets Coach Ken Hitchcock. "I'd watch him in the warmup. He transcends. I think he's the evolution of our game."

HOME AND FAMILY

Ovechkin owns a home near Arlington, Virginia, that he often shares with his brother and parents. He spends his summers in Moscow.

HOBBIES AND OTHER INTERESTS

In his spare time, Ovechkin likes to relax by playing cards, watching movies, and playing video games. He gives back to the community through a program called Ovi's Crazy Eights. He purchases eight tickets to every Capitals home game and donates them to needy children or U.S. soldiers and their families. The group sits in a special section and receives free souvenirs, and Ovechkin pays them a personal visit after the game. The Ovi's Crazy Eights program also donates money to Russian orphanages and to Right to Play, an international charity that uses sports to help disadvantaged children.

HONORS AND AWARDS

Calder Memorial Trophy (NHL Rookie of the Year): 2006
NHL All-Star Team: 2006, 2007, 2008, 2009
Kharlamov Trophy (Best Russian Player in the NHL): 2006, 2007, 2008, 2009
Hart Trophy (NHL Most Valuable Player): 2008, 2009

Lester B. Pearson Award (outstanding NHL player as voted by peers): 2008, 2009
Maurice "Rocket" Richard Trophy (most goals in NHL season): 2008, 2009
Art Ross Trophy (most points in NHL season): 2008

FURTHER READING

Periodicals

Current Biography Yearbook, 2008
Hamilton Spectator (Ontario, Canada), Apr. 8, 2008, p.SP10
New York Times, Oct. 1, 2006; Feb. 13, 2008; Feb. 22, 2009
Sporting News, Sep. 29, 2006, p.14; Sep. 29, 2008, p.50; Mar. 16, 2009, p.62; May 25, 2009, p.10
Tampa Tribune, Mar. 27, 2008, p.1
USA Today, Oct. 18, 2005, p.C10; Dec. 7, 2005, p.C1; Feb. 3, 2006, p.C13
Washington Post, June 13, 2008, p.E1

Online Articles

http://www.canada.com
(Canada.com, "Ovechkin: NHL Fans' Plan B," Apr. 12, 2008)
http://sports.espn.go.com
(ESPN, "Ovechkin Confident of His Arrival," May 30, 2004)
http://www.nhl.com
(NHL, "Cheers, Jeers for Ovechkin Celebration," Mar. 20, 2009)
http://sportsillustrated.cnn.com
(Sports Illustrated, "Q&A: Alexander Ovechkin," Feb. 16, 2007)
http://www.washingtonpost.com
(Washington Post, "The Great Ones Get It," May 6, 2009)

ADDRESS

Alexander Ovechkin
Washington Capitals
627 North Glebe Road, Ste. 850
Arlington, VA 22203

WORLD WIDE WEB SITES

http://www.alexovechkin8.com
http://capitals.nhl.com
http://www.nhl.com

Brad Paisley 1972-

American Country Singer, Songwriter, and Guitarist
Named Top Male Vocalist by the Country Music Association and the Academy of Country Music

BIRTH

Brad Douglas Paisley was born October 28, 1972, in the small town of Glen Dale, West Virginia, located on the Ohio River. He was the only child of Doug Paisley, who worked for the West Virginia Department of Transportation, and Sandy Jarvis Paisley, a teacher.

YOUTH

Paisley had a very close bond with his maternal grandfather, Warren Jarvis, who lived nearby. Jarvis was a railroad employee who worked the night shift. Because he was home in the afternoons, his grandson spent a lot of time at his house. "He was the best friend I ever had," Paisley has said. Jarvis was an enthusiastic guitar player who loved traditional country music. He often sat for hours on his porch, playing one song after another.

When Paisley was eight years old, his grandfather gave him a Sears Danelectro Silvertone guitar and began teaching him how to play. Learning can be difficult at first, as it requires holding the hands in some uncomfortable positions. "I kind of fought it for a while, 'cause at eight you'd rather play sports or do anything other than something that hurts your hand," Paisley recalled. "But the thing that kept me going was knowing how bad he wanted me to do that. I think he enjoyed it so much he wanted me to be able to have that in my life. He changed my life in a way no one ever will again."

When Paisley was eight years old, his grandfather began teaching him how to play guitar. "I kind of fought it for a while, 'cause at eight you'd rather play sports or do anything other than something that hurts your hand," Paisley recalled. "But the thing that kept me going was knowing how bad he wanted me to do that. I think he enjoyed it so much he wanted me to be able to have that in my life. He changed my life in a way no one ever will again."

Paisley gave his first public performance when he was 10 years old, singing at church. His hometown audience was very supportive of the young musician. "Pretty soon, I was performing at every Christmas party and Mother's Day event," he remembered. "The neat thing about a small town is that when you want to be an artist, by golly, they'll make you one." At the age of 12, Paisley wrote his first composition, "Born on Christmas Day." By that time, he had started taking lessons with a local guitarist, Clarence "Hank" Goddard. Recognizing Paisley's great potential, Goddard gave his student a lot of encouragement, and a thorough grounding in the basics. By the time Paisley was 13 years old, he and Goddard had formed a band called Brad Paisley and the C-Notes. Two of Goddard's other friends, both seasoned, adult musicians, filled out the group.

Regular on Radio

When Paisley was in junior high school, his principal heard him perform "Born on Christmas Day" and invited him to play at a meeting of the local Rotary Club. At that meeting was Tom Miller, the program director at a radio station in nearby Wheeling, West Virginia. Miller asked Paisley if he'd like to be a guest on "Jamboree USA," a program that aired on Saturday nights. The show was legendary in the area, and Paisley was thrilled to accept. "I ran through the house screaming, 'I'm going to play the Jamboree!'" he said. "My grandfather was just super-proud. All of a sudden, he was seeing this guitar he'd given to me become my life."

After his first appearance, Paisley was asked to become a member of the show's weekly lineup. For the next eight years, he opened the show for some of the biggest acts in country music. He eventually became the youngest person ever inducted into the Jamboree USA Hall of Fame. He was also part of the regular lineup at Jamboree in the Hills, a famous outdoor music festival held near Wheeling. His experiences on the radio show and at the festival were invaluable in learning about both the artistic side and the business side of music. About two months before his grandfather died, Paisley was asked to go on tour with the Judds, one of the most popular acts in country music. "He got to see that," Paisley said of his grandfather. "It was like giving Moses a look at the Promised Land. He knew that guitar was the best gift I ever received."

EDUCATION

By the time he started high school, Paisley had an extensive background in traditional gospel and country music and was performing regularly with world-famous entertainers. Still, he was able to pick up more musical knowledge at John Marshall High School in Glen Dale. Playing in the school's jazz band exposed him to a kind of music he never heard at home, and listening to music with his friends introduced him to rock bands that were new to him, like Pink Floyd and U2. He'd listen to the different kinds of music, then try to play what he heard. These influences gave depth to his developing musicianship.

After graduating from high school in 1991, Paisley started classes at West Liberty State College, about 20 miles from his home town. He went there for two years before transferring to Belmont University in Nashville, Tennessee. Nashville is the capital of country music, and Paisley's time there was valuable not only for what he learned in his courses, but also for the friends and business contacts he made. He had internships at ASCAP (the American Society of Composers, Authors & Publishers), Atlantic Records,

Paisley's first album, Who Needs Pictures, *featured a traditional country sound.*

and the Fitzgerald-Hartley management firm. He also made friends with other young people who would become his partners in writing and producing many albums—Frank Rogers, Chris DuBois, and Kelley Lovelace, among others. In 1995, Paisley graduated from Belmont with a bachelor's degree in music business.

CAREER HIGHLIGHTS

Within a week of his college graduation, Paisley had signed a deal with EMI to work as a songwriter. Songwriters frequently record demos of their compositions for vocalists to preview, and Paisley turned out many of these. His first hit was "Another You," as recorded by David Kersh. Before long, the strength of Paisley's demos led executives at Arista Records to offer him his own contract as a recording artist. Paisley was only 26 years old, but he had years of experience behind him and an excellent grasp of what elements were needed for success in the music business. "Brad came to the table with very concrete, very well-thought ideas of what should be done at every level," recalled Mike Dungan, a senior vice-president and general manager at Arista. "I'm not talking about an uneducated kid here. I'm talking about somebody who came to the table with really great ideas."

Who Needs Pictures

Paisley had never recorded an album before, yet he had enough confidence to do things his own way. He insisted on using his own band and on playing all the guitar tracks himself, rather than using studio musicians as is usual for recording sessions. Instead of hiring an experienced producer, he hired his friend from college, Frank Rogers. While Rogers was inexperienced, Paisley had faith in his talent and in their ability to work together. Drawing from their large backlog of compositions, they began work on Paisley's album in 1998.

On June 1, 1999, *Who Needs Pictures* was released. Featuring a traditional country sound, impressive guitar work, and strong lyrics, *Who Needs Pictures* was an immediate success. The album yielded two chart-topping country singles, the romantic "We Danced" and "He Didn't Have to Be." The lyrics of "He Didn't Have to Be," co-written with Kelley Lovelace and telling the story of a man who cares enough to be a good father to a child who isn't his own, were inspired by the relationship between Lovelace and his stepson. "He Didn't Have to Be" spent two weeks at the top of the country singles charts and was nominated as Song of the Year and Single of the Year by the Country Music Association. Both awards ended up going to other artists, but it was significant even to be nominated. Strong sales of *Who Needs Pictures* continued long after its initial release. By February 2001, it was certified platinum, meaning it had sold more than one million copies.

> "
>
> *When Paisley was in junior high school, he was asked to be a guest on "Jamboree USA," a program that aired on Saturday nights and was legendary in the area. "I ran through the house screaming, 'I'm going to play the Jamboree!'" he said. "My grandfather was just super-proud. All of a sudden, he was seeing this guitar he'd given to me become my life."*
>
> "

Paisley humbly receives the Grand Ole Opry Member Award after being inducted into the Opry in 2001.

Youngest Member of the Grand Ole Opry

On May 28, 1999, just before the release of *Who Needs Pictures,* Paisley was asked to make an appearance at the Grand Ole Opry, a weekly concert and radio broadcast originating from Nashville, Tennessee. First broadcast on the Nashville radio station WSM in 1925, the Grand Ole Opry has long been an important institution in country music, showcasing classic acts alongside rising stars. After making about 40 appearances on the show, Paisley was invited to become a member of the Opry on February 17, 2001. This invitation is a great honor, given only to those who represent the best in country music. If accepted, artists must keep their membership active by making numerous appearances at the Opry throughout the year. Paisley was 28 years old when he accepted the invitation, making him the youngest member of the Opry.

Paisley's close association with the Opry showed his dedication to country music's roots. His story songs and humorous numbers were very traditional, yet his music also featured a strong guitar sound that was fresh and appealing. The Grand Ole Opry had lost some of its influence over the years, as more and more crossover artists came to dominate the country music scene. Traditionalists were thrilled to have one of country's hottest young stars become a member of the Opry. When the CBS television network produced a special in honor of the Opry's 75th anniversary, Paisley and

Chely Wright performed a duet called "Hard to Be a Husband, Hard to Be a Wife," written especially for the show. Released in 2000 on the album *Backstage at the Opry,* the duet was nominated for the Vocal Event of the Year award at 2001 Country Music Association Awards.

Part II

Recording artists sometimes have a tough time following up a sensational debut like *Who Needs Pictures,* but Paisley had no such problem. In fact, he visualized his second album as the sequel, and the title, *Part II,* reflected this. To emphasize the continuity between the two albums, *Part II* even begins with fiddle music that was the last sound heard on *Who Needs Pictures*. Released in 2001, *Part II* was on the *Billboard* country albums charts for more than 70 weeks and was certified platinum in August of that year. Paisley supported the album by touring as the opening act for Lonestar, a popular modern country group, and by performing at fairs and summer music festivals around the country.

Part II had two singles reach the top of the country charts, "I Wish You'd Stay" and "I'm Gonna Miss Her (The Fishin' Song)." Two other singles, "Wrapped Around" and "Two People Fell in Love," also charted in the country Top 10. The No. 1 singles showed Paisley's diversity: "I Wish You'd Stay" was a wistful number about saying good-bye to a loved one, while "I'm Gonna Miss Her" is a tongue-in-cheek song about a man whose girlfriend tells him she'll leave him if he doesn't stop spending so much time fishing. As he sits in his boat waiting for a nibble on his line, he reflects that she will be missed. "I'm Gonna Miss Her" became one of Paisley's signature songs, and it also had special significance in his personal life. While casting the video for the song, Paisley thought of Kimberly Williams, an actress he'd seen some years before in the movie *Father of the Bride.* He asked her to play the part of the girlfriend in the video, and she and Paisley began dating in real life. They were married in 2003.

Mainstream Success and Multiple Awards

Paisley's third album, *Mud on the Tires,* came out in 2003. It topped the *Billboard* country album charts and was certified double platinum, meaning it sold more than two million copies. *Mud on the Tires* was Paisley's first album to make it into the Top 10 of the general album charts as well. "I'm Gonna Miss Her" had firmly established Paisley as a funny singer in many peoples' minds. While he appreciated the success of his song, he didn't like being pigeonholed. "It's sort of an insult," he remarked. "To me, part of entertaining is trying to capture all the various experiences. I'm a big fan of

In concert, Paisley offers an elaborate stage show to create a memorable experience for concert-goers.

... [artists] like the Beatles—from single to single, you didn't know where they were going next. Nothing makes me want to go do a really dark album more than the people who say,'You're all about funny.'"

One of the most popular tunes from *Mud on the Tires* showed Paisley's darker side. "Whiskey Lullaby," written by Jon Randall and Bill Anderson, told a grim tale of a love gone wrong and the man and woman who drink themselves to death over it. Paisley recorded it as a duet with Alison Krauss, an acclaimed bluegrass vocalist. The song and the dramatic video made for it got a lot of attention. The album brought Paisley more Grammy nominations than any other male artist that year, but he still didn't win, in any category.

That changed after the release of his fourth album, *Time Well Wasted,* which came out in 2005. *Time Well Wasted* again demonstrated Paisley's range, containing both funny and serious songs. One standout from the album was "When I Get Where I'm Going," an uplifting gospel duet with Dolly Parton, one of country's most respected female stars. A completely different tone was struck with "Alcohol," which was nominated for a Grammy Award. "Whiskey Lullaby" had portrayed the tragic and fatal effects of drinking, but "Alcohol" was more lighthearted, while still pointing out alcohol's negative effects. The lyrics are written from the point of view of the alcohol itself, including the line, "You had some of the best times you'll never remember with me, alcohol." *Time Well Wasted* eventually went double platinum and was awarded Album of the Year honors by both the Academy of Country Music and the Country Music Association.

"With each song I choose, I have to visualize the people in the front rows of my shows enjoying it as we perform it," Paisley said. "If I can see them singing along, smiling and laughing, or holding up a lighter or cell phone, then the song is a keeper."

”

As his popularity continued to increase, Paisley remained down-to-earth, giving lots of credit for his success to his songwriting collaborators, his backing musicians, and his recording crew. After winning the Country Music Association's Album of the Year award for *Time Well Wasted,* he brought the trophy into the recording studio to share with everyone there. "We gave each other a round of applause, and I told everybody,'Congratulations, this is yours. Now, let's do even better.' That's the mindset we had," he recalled. "I didn't mean that we expect to win it again. What I meant was, 'Let's see if we can top it.' We wanted to aim at pushing ourselves and at doing something we felt moved the music forward."

Moving ahead in High Gear

Paisley's next major album was *5th Gear,* released in 2007. The title is not only a reference to it being his fifth major album, but also to the fifth gear used in driving. Fifth gear "is something you reach when you're on a long, good stretch and you're really rolling," he said. "This album, and this time in my career, feels like that. We are pushing things further in every way—musically, lyrically, and in our concerts."

5th Gear reached No. 1 on the country charts and No. 3 on the general album charts. It yielded five No. 1 country singles: "Ticks," "Online," "Letter to Me," "I'm Still a Guy," and "Throttleneck," a hard-driving instrumental that won Paisley his first Grammy Award. In "Letter to Me," the lyrics reflect on the singer's younger self, a theme that runs through the entire project. "Online" was a funny number about the way people misrepresent themselves when chatting online. "Ticks" was another humorous song, about a guy trying to charm a girl by inviting her to take a romantic walk in the woods, reassuring her that he'll make sure she hasn't been bitten by any ticks when they're done walking. "If you think this song is gross, you're missing the point," he said. "It's not about bloodsucking bugs. It's about a guy flirting with a girl, and, in trying to tell her he's interested in her, he's using a term that's about as country as can be."

In 2007, Paisley was recognized with Male Vocalist of the Year honors from both the Country Music Association and the Academy of Country Music. That year he produced a more expensive and elaborate stage show that featured the music from *5th Gear.* Paisley loves to use cutting-edge technology to create a memorable experience for concert-goers. He always keeps his live shows in mind during the process of writing and selecting songs for albums. "With each song I choose, I have to visualize the people in the front rows of my shows enjoying it as we perform it," he said. "If I can see them singing along, smiling and laughing, or holding up a lighter or cell phone, then the song is a keeper." The tour ran from April 2007 through February 2008, stopping in 94 cities and attracting more than one million fans.

In 2008, Paisley followed *5th Gear* with *Play,* an album of mostly instrumental music. He had earned a reputation as one of the best guitarists in country music, but Paisley knew that instrumental albums are rarely

Paisley's most recent release, American Saturday Night, *includes "Welcome to the Future," the song that he says is his personal favorite.*

as popular as vocal music. He didn't mind. "Many of my fans have probably never bought a jazz album or a true blues album," he said, "so it was a challenge to make something that's not a complete disaster to them. I wanted *Play* to be something that people who never bought an instrumental record of any kind before would have a good time listening to." *Play* featured duets with Keith Urban and Vince Gill, two other country artists known for their guitar skills, as well as the legendary blues musician B.B. King and other top musicians. The result was a "risky, thrilling" album, according to *Guitar Player* reviewer Jude Gold. It was also another hit with Paisley's audience, debuting at the top of the country album charts.

American Saturday Night

After taking an instrumental break on *Play,* Paisley geared up for his next album, *American Saturday Night.* As usual, it was a group effort. "I rely on these guys that I trust like Chris [DuBois], Frank [Rogers] and Tim Owens, Kelley Lovelace, Ashley Gorley, and Bill Anderson—all these guys that throughout the years have become family," he said. "It's truly just a team now." *American Saturday Night* was released in 2009, at a time when many Americans were struggling with the effects of global economic problems. The overall tone of the album expressed hope and gratitude, even in the face of tough times. The first single released, a ballad called "Then," became Paisley's 14th No. 1 country hit, and his 10th No. 1 single in a row.

"Paisley remains humble about his talent and his success. "I've really not been good at much else," he remarked. "Thankfully I was able to do this for a living because … I did not have anything to fall back on, that's for sure.""

The title track evoked a picture of Americans working hard through the week and looking forward to a bit of freedom on the weekends. "Water" celebrated summer fun, and "The Pants" was a wry look at relationships. "Welcome to the Future," which Paisley wrote with Bill Anderson, is the songwriter's personal favorite and the one he feels is the most important. It was inspired by the 2008 election of Barack Obama as president of the United States. Paisley was very moved that, after years of racism, the country was ready to accept an African American as its leader. The lyrics express wonder at how quickly things can change, referring to rapid advancements in technology, shifting relationships between countries, and improvements in civil rights.

On July 21, 2009, Paisley was one of a group of entertainers invited to be part of the White House Music Series launched by First Lady Michelle Obama. The series was designed to encourage the arts and arts education, and included a music workshop with the invited performers. Alison Krauss, Paisley's partner on the "Whiskey Lullaby" duet, was another of the musicians who took part. The artists later had the opportunity to perform for President Barack Obama, Michelle Obama, the White House staff, and members of Congress.

Paisley was honored to be part of a group of performers invited to perform at the White House by First Lady Michelle Obama.

Despite selling millions of albums, touring the world, and being invited to perform at the White House, Paisley remains humble about his talent and his success. "I've really not been good at much else," he remarked. "Thankfully I was able to do this for a living because … I did not have anything to fall back on, that's for sure."

HOME AND FAMILY

Paisley lives with his wife, Kimberly Williams-Paisley, and their two sons, William Huckleberry and Jasper Warren. William Huckleberry's middle name was taken from Mark Twain's classic American novel *Huckleberry Finn,* and his parents call him by his nickname, "Huck." Jasper Warren's name honors Paisley's guitar-playing grandfather.

The family has two homes. Williams-Paisley is a co-star of the television comedy "According to Jim," which is taped in Los Angeles, California, where they have a home. Paisley prefers to spend time at their other residence, which is a big log home on 87 acres in Franklin, Tennessee. There they do some farming and keep horses and other animals, including a Cavalier King Charles Spaniel named Holler.

HOBBIES AND OTHER INTERESTS

Paisley has a large collection of exotic and vintage guitars. He enjoys matching the various sounds they produce to the songs he's working on.

His favorite guitar is a 1968 Fender Telecaster. The fret board is made of maple wood, and it's decorated with a paisley design. He loves gadgets and new technology and has taught himself to use animation software and other tools to create videos that enhance his stage shows. He likes many outdoor activities, including horseback riding, fishing, and hunting with bow and rifle.

From 2003 until 2005, Paisley was on the national board of advisors of Mothers Against Drunk Driving (MADD). He formed the Brad Paisley Foundation to benefit charities such as the Children's Miracle Network, St. Jude's Research Hospital, the Opry Trust Fund, and the American Cancer Society.

RECORDINGS

Who Needs Pictures, 1999
Backstage at the Opry, 2000 (contributor)
Part II, 2001
Mud on the Tires, 2003
Time Well Wasted, 2005
Brad Paisley Christmas, 2006
Cars, 2006 (contributor to soundtrack)
5th Gear, 2007
Play, 2008
American Saturday Night, 2009

SELECTED HONORS AND AWARDS

Academy of Country Music Awards: 2000, Top New Male Vocalist of the Year; 2005 (2 awards), Vocal Event of the Year and Video of the Year, both for "Whiskey Lullaby" (with Alison Krauss); 2006 (3 awards), Album of the Year, for *Time Well Wasted,* and Vocal Event of the Year and Video Event of the Year, both for "When I Get Where I'm Going" (with Dolly Parton); 2007, Top Male Vocalist of the Year; 2008 (2 awards), Top Male Vocalist of the Year, and Video of the Year, for "Online"; 2009 (2 awards), Video of the Year, for "Waitin' on a Woman," and Vocal Event of the Year, for "Start a Band" (with Keith Urban)

Country Music Association Awards: 2000, Horizon Award; 2001, Vocal Event of the Year, for "Too Country" (with Buck Owens, George Jones, and Bill Anderson); 2002, Music Video of the Year, for "I'm Gonna Miss Her (The Fishin' Song)"; 2004 (2 awards), Music Video of the Year and Musical Event of the Year, both for "Whiskey Lullaby" (with Alison Krauss); 2006 (2 awards), Album of the Year, for *Time Well Wasted,* and Musical Event of the Year, for "When I Get Where I'm Going" (with

Dolly Parton); 2007 (2 awards), Male Vocalist of the Year and Music Video of the Year, for "Online"; 2008 (2 awards), Male Vocalist of the Year and Music Video of the Year, for "Waitin' on a Woman"
Orville H. Gibson Guitar Award for Best Country Guitarist (Male): 2002
Nashville Songwriters Association International Award for Song-writer/Artist of the Year: 2002, 2005
CMT/Flameworthy Music Awards: 2002, Flameworthy Concept Video of the Year, for "I'm Gonna Miss Her (The Fishin' Song)"; 2005, CMT Music Award for Collaborative Video of the Year, for "Whiskey Lullaby" (with Alison Krauss); 2006, CMT Award for Most Inspiring Video of the Year, for "When I Get Where I'm Going" (with Dolly Parton); 2008, Comedy Video of the Year, for "Online"; 2009 (3 awards), Male Video of the Year, for "Waitin' on a Woman," Collaborative Video of the Year, for "Start a Band" (with Keith Urban), and CMT Performance of the Year, for "Country Boy"
ASCAP Country Music Award: 2004, Songwriter/Artist of the Year
Grammy Awards (The Recording Academy): 2008, Best Country Instrumental Performance, for "Throttleneck"; 2009 (2 awards), Best Country Instrumental Performance, for "Cluster Pluck" (with James Burton, Vince Gill, Albert Lee, John Jorgenson, Brent Mason, Redd Volkaert, and Steve Wariner) and Best Male Country Vocal Performance, for "Letter to Me"
American Music Award: 2008, Favorite Country Male Artist

FURTHER READING

Periodicals

Billboard, Aug. 16, 2003, p.31; June 2, 2007, p.28; May 16, 2009, p.17
Boston Globe, July 5, 2009, p.N5
Entertainment Weekly, Aug. 24, 2007, p.27
Good Housekeeping, Jan. 2008, p.122
Guitar Player, Dec. 2007, p.78; Mar. 2009, p.74
USA Today, Aug. 8, 2007, p.D8

Online Articles

http://www.cmt.com/artists
(CMT, "Brad Paisley," no date)
http://www.people.com/people/brad_paisley
(People, "Celebrity Central: Brad Paisley," no date)
http://www.washingtonpost.com
(Washington Post, "White House Goes a Little Bit Country," July 21, 2009)

ADDRESS

Brad Paisley
Arista Nashville
1400 18th Ave. South
Nashville, TN 37212

WORLD WIDE WEB SITES

http://www.bradpaisley.com

Candace Parker 1986-

American Professional Basketball Player with the Los Angeles Sparks
WNBA Rookie of the Year and Most Valuable Player in 2008

BIRTH

Candace Nicole Parker was born on April 19, 1986, in St. Louis, Missouri. Her father, Larry Parker, is in the insurance business. Her mother, Sara Parker, works in the front office for the WNBA's Chicago Sky. Candace is the youngest of three children in her family. Her brother Anthony, who is 11 years older, plays guard for the NBA's Toronto Raptors. Her brother Marcus, who is eight years older, is a doctor.

YOUTH

Candace grew up in Naperville, Illinois, about 25 miles southwest of Chicago. Her whole family loved basketball, so she learned about the game from an early age. Her father played at the University of Iowa in the 1970s, and her brother Anthony was a standout player at the high school, college, and professional levels. Candace first attended one of her brother's games when she was just two weeks old.

The Parkers were also big fans of the Chicago Bulls professional team, which won six National Basketball Association (NBA) championships between 1991 and 1999. "[Candace has] been in the gym her whole life, and I think that's helped her basketball IQ," her mother noted. "We used to take her to Bulls games when she was five years old, and she would make comments like, 'If they're going to win this game, somebody's going to have to start rebounding! Somebody needs to box out!' She understood the game even then."

"

"If me and my dad went to a park and he didn't think I was practicing hard enough, he'd just get in the car and leave," Parker remembered. "And I'd have to run home. I mean run home. Once I figured that out, I'd always try to go to close-by parks."

"

Although Candace understood basketball, she was initially reluctant to play the game. She worried that she would always be compared to her father and brother. This concern led her to focus her athletic talents on soccer until she reached the eighth grade. By that time, however, she had grown so tall that her parents encouraged her to switch sports. As soon as she started playing organized basketball, Candace proved to be a natural on the court. She also worked hard to improve her skills and often tested herself by playing against her bigger, stronger brothers.

Candace's father became her coach, as well as her toughest critic. "He did things to make me mad, to challenge me, because I was so much more athletic and had so much more knowledge of the game than everyone else that sometimes I just coasted," Candace recalled. Her father always pushed her to do her best, even in practice. They spent countless hours at local parks doing rigorous drills to improve her shooting, ball handling, and passing skills. "If me and my dad went to a park and he didn't think I was practicing hard enough, he'd just get in the car and leave," she remembered. "And I'd have to run home. I mean run home. Once I figured that out, I'd always try to go to close-by parks."

Parker won the slam dunk contest at the 2004 McDonald's High School All-American Game, the first girl ever to win that event.

EDUCATION

Parker attended Naperville Central High School, where she became the star player on the powerful Lady Redhawks basketball team. During her sophomore year, she came to national attention by becoming the first female high-school player—and only the fifth woman at any level—to dunk a basketball during a sanctioned game. "The first two times I tried it in games I failed. Embarrassing," Parker recalled. "The third time was a charm, and then cameras and reporters were everywhere—everyone wanted to talk about dunking."

In March 2004, during her senior year of high school, Parker became the first girl ever to win the slam-dunk contest at the annual McDonald's High School All-American Game. She defeated some of the top male players in the country, including two future NBA first-round draft picks. "It was special, but that's not what I want to be known for," she said. "Eventually the hype about my dunks will die down because more women players will do it."

Parker proved herself to be an outstanding all-around player throughout her high-school career. She averaged 22.9 points and 13.2 rebounds per game and led her team to consecutive Class AA Illinois state championships in 2003 and 2004. She received several major national awards following both her junior and senior seasons, including the Naismith Prep Player of the Year, Gatorade High School Player of the Year, and *USA Today* Player of the Year awards. By the time she graduated in 2004 with a 3.7 grade-point average, Parker was the most highly recruited player in the country. When she signed a letter of intent to play college basketball for the University of Tennessee Lady Volunteers, the signing ceremony was broadcast live on ESPN.

University of Tennessee Lady Volunteers

Parker was thrilled to go to Nashville and play for legendary Tennessee basketball coach Pat Summitt, who had won more games than any other National Collegiate Athletic Association (NCAA) Division I coach in history. (For more information on Summitt, see *Biography Today Sports,* Vol. 3.) Shortly before the start of her freshman year, however, Parker underwent surgery to repair an injured left knee. After several unsuccessful attempts to come back from the surgery, she reluctantly agreed to sit out the 2004-05 season. "In my head I knew I shouldn't play, but my heart wanted to," she admitted. Parker received a special status called a "redshirt," which meant that she still retained four years of eligibility to play college basketball. Although she felt deeply disappointed about missing the season, Parker worked hard at knee rehabilitation and other training exercises. She added 10 pounds of muscle to her six foot, five inch frame and increased her vertical leap to an impressive 27 inches.

“

"She's the toughest matchup in the game," said University of Mississippi Coach Carol Ross. "On many nights, she's the best guard on the floor, the best post on the floor, the best rebounder on the floor, the best passer on the floor and, let's not forget, the best scorer on the floor. She's got the strut of a competitor and the stuff of a champion."

”

Parker made her long-awaited college debut during the 2005-06 season. Although she was listed as a forward on the team roster, she also played center and guard. From the beginning, opposing coaches struggled to find a way to defend against her. "She's the toughest matchup in the game," said University of Mississippi Coach Carol Ross. "On many nights, she's the best guard on the floor, the best post on the floor, the best rebounder on the floor, the best passer on the floor and, let's not forget, the best scorer on the floor. She's got the strut of a competitor and the stuff of a champion." On March 19, 2006, Parker made history once again by becoming the first woman ever to dunk twice in an NCAA game.

During her second season (2006-07), Parker led the Lady Vols to their first NCAA championship since 1998. Parker's strong performance earned her

Parker, a three-time All-American and 2008 Naismith Player of the Year, helped the Lady Vols to National Championships in 2007 and 2008 before becoming the number one draft pick in the WNBA. She holds the school record with seven career dunks.

Most Valuable Player honors in the NCAA tournament, as well as the John R. Wooden Award as the nation's top female college player. She came back in 2007-08 to help Tennessee claim a second consecutive national title. In addition to earning tournament MVP honors for the second straight year, Parker also claimed the Naismith Player of the Year Award and won the prestigious Honda-Broderick Cup as the Collegiate Female Athlete of the Year.

In February 2008 Parker announced that she planned to give up her fourth year of college eligibility to play professionally in the Women's National Basketball Association (WNBA). "My experience here at Tennessee has been great. I look back at my growth, not only as a player but also just as a person, and I feel like it's been the best four years of my life. I wouldn't change anything," she stated. "It was a difficult decision for me to forego my senior year, but I just felt like it was the right decision to make going out as a champion." Parker completed her time at Tennessee with career averages of 19.4 points, 8.8 rebounds, and 2.2 blocks per game—and a college diploma as well. A two-time Academic All-American, she earned a bachelor's degree in sports management in May 2008.

CAREER HIGHLIGHTS

WNBA: The Los Angeles Sparks

Parker was selected first overall in the 2008 WNBA draft by the Los Angeles Sparks. The Sparks had a proud history—they won back-to-back WNBA championships in 2001 and 2002. But the team had posted a league-worst 10-24 record in 2007. The Sparks' star player, veteran center Lisa Leslie, had given birth to her first child and missed the entire season. In her absence, Los Angeles failed to make the playoffs for the first time in nine years.

Parker made her professional debut for the Sparks on May 17, 2008. Playing against the defending WNBA champion Phoenix Mercury, she scored 34 points, grabbed 12 rebounds, and dished out 8 assists. She set a new record for points scored by a WNBA rookie in her very first game. "It obviously was better than I expected," she acknowledged. "Coming out, I just wanted to play hard. I was a little nervous, and I think my teammates did a good job of just keeping me in it mentally and not allowing me to get frustrated."

Another highlight of Parker's rookie season came on June 22, when she became the second player ever to dunk in a WNBA game (the first was her teammate Lisa Leslie in 2002). "When I caught the ball and there was an open lane, it was a good opportunity," she recalled. "I'm happy that I was able to do it in Los Angeles in front of the home fans."

In August the WNBA suspended play for a few weeks to allow some of the league's star players to join the U.S. national women's basketball team at the 2008 Summer Olympic Games in Beijing, China. Parker was delighted to be invited to represent the United States in the Olympics. She and her teammates breezed through the Olympic basketball tournament, winning eight straight games by an average margin of 38.8 points. Team USA defeated Australia by a score of 92-65 to win the gold medal. Parker averaged 9.4 points per game in the Olympic tournament and contributed 14 points in the gold medal game.

Parker has expressed confidence that she can balance her career and her family life. "There's room for basketball, there's room for Lailaa," she explained. "I have, from a young age, said I wanted both. I want a career and I want a family and I wasn't going to have to choose. Right now I'm living my dream because I have the best of both worlds. I go to basketball and I love it and I play and then I come home and there's that joy."

"

After returning to the Sparks, Parker resumed her fantastic rookie season. She led her team to a 20-14 record and a spot in the playoffs. The Sparks beat the Seattle Storm in the Western Conference semifinals, but lost to the San Antonio Silver Stars in the conference finals. Parker's season averages of 18.5 points and 9.5 rebounds per game made her an easy choice for WNBA Rookie of the Year honors. She also earned the league's Most Valuable Player Award, thus becoming the first player in WNBA history to win both awards in the same season.

To cap off one of the greatest individual years in the history of women's basketball, Parker was named Female Athlete of the Year by the Associated Press. "She enjoyed an incredible run," Coach Summitt said of Parker's 2008 NCAA title, Olympic gold medal, and prestigious awards. "It was an exceptional year for an exceptional athlete and person."

Balancing Career and Family

Parker's remarkable season drew the attention of basketball fans across the country. The Sparks attracted huge crowds wherever they played, and the WNBA's TV ratings increased by 19 percent for the 2008 season. Parker quickly established herself as one of the most popular players in the league, and her number 3 Sparks jersey became the WNBA's top seller.

"When I see little girls wearing them it reminds me of when I was little at Bulls games and I wanted Ron Harper's jersey and autograph," she said. "To think someone feels that way about me is so flattering. It means the women's game is growing and it's a great time for me to be involved in the evolution of the game." In recognition of her appeal to fans, Parker received lucrative endorsement deals with Adidas and Gatorade.

In January 2009 Parker's personal life became the center of public attention. She announced that she and her husband of two months, Boston Celtics center Shelden Williams, were expecting a baby in the spring. Although they had not planned to start a family so soon, they looked forward to welcoming the new baby. "I was surprised," Parker admitted. "But everything happens for a reason. It will be exciting to have my child share my career and to remember what I was like when I was young."

The news of Parker's pregnancy came as a shock to her teammates, sponsors, and fans. Some critics questioned her commitment to her basketball career. Others called her careless or selfish. But WNBA commissioner Donna Orender defended Parker's right to make her own decisions. "It's the miracle of life, and it doesn't always happen on your time schedule," she said. "That's how it goes, you know? Parker will come back—and we'll have one more fan." Parker gave birth to a daughter, Lailaa, in May 2009. She missed the first eight games of the 2009 WNBA season.

Returning to the Court

While Parker was absent at the beginning of the 2009 season, the Sparks posted a 3-5 record. She returned to the court just seven weeks after giving birth and quickly regained her old form. By season's end she had registered 13.1 points, 9.8 rebounds, and 2.6 assists per game. Her contributions helped boost the Sparks to an 18-16 record and a spot in the playoffs. But the Sparks' hopes of capturing the WNBA title ended in disappointment. Parker and her teammates defeated the Seattle Storm in the Western Conference semifinals, but they lost to the Phoenix Mercury in the conference finals.

After Parker took time off to have a baby, some people have questioned whether motherhood would limit her basketball career. But Parker has expressed confidence that she can balance her career and her family life. "There's room for basketball, there's room for Lailaa," she explained. "I have, from a young age, said I wanted both. I want a career and I want a family and I wasn't going to have to choose. Right now I'm living my dream because I have the best of both worlds. I go to basketball and I love it and I play and then I come home and there's that joy."

Parker goes up against Phoenix Mercury guard Diana Taurasi during the 2009 WNBA Western Conference finals, which the Mercury ultimately won.

Parker also hopes to set a good example for her daughter, as well as for her many young fans. "Now everything I do is for my daughter," she noted. "She's going to be watching and I take that mindset with me. I want to be a good role model for her, show her girls can do anything guys can do."

MARRIAGE AND FAMILY

Parker first met her husband, NBA player Shelden Williams, when she made an official recruiting visit to Duke University during high school. Williams was a sophomore at Duke and a star player on the Blue Devils men's basketball team at the time. They started dating two years later, when Parker and the Lady Volunteers came to Duke to play a game. They got married on November 13, 2008. "When I was getting ready to propose," Williams remembered, "she kept jamming her finger, and I could never get her actual ring size. So I got a special ring with a clasp at the bottom that allows her to open it and put it over her finger, so that no matter what happens to her knuckle, it'll always fit." Their daughter, Lailaa, was born on May 13, 2009.

HOBBIES AND OTHER INTERESTS

In her spare time, Parker likes to relax by walking her two dogs. She also enjoys watching old TV comedies like "Full House" and "The Cosby Show." Parker has performed community service work with a number of organizations, including D.A.R.E., Loaves and Fishes, and the Ronald McDonald House.

HONORS AND AWARDS

Illinois Miss Basketball: 2002, 2003, 2004
Gatorade High School Player of the Year: 2003, 2004
Naismith Prep Player of the Year: 2003, 2004
USA Today High School Player of the Year: 2003, 2004
Southeastern Conference Rookie of the Year: 2006
Kodak All-American: 2006, 2007, 2008
John R. Wooden Player of the Year: 2007, 2008
NCAA Women's Basketball Tournament Most Outstanding Player: 2007, 2008
Academic All-American: 2008
Naismith Player of the Year: 2008
Honda-Broderick Cup: 2008
Olympic Women's Basketball: 2008, gold medal
WNBA Rookie of the Year: 2008
WNBA Most Valuable Player: 2008
Female Athlete of the Year (Associated Press): 2008

FURTHER READING

Books

Ross, Alan. *Second to None: The National Championship Teams of the Tennessee Lady Vols,* 2009

Periodicals

ESPN The Magazine, Mar. 23, 2009 (cover story)
Jet, Oct. 20, 2003, p.54; Apr. 28, 2008, p.48
New York Times, Jan. 23, 2004; Apr. 1, 2004; Apr. 4, 2007; Aug. 18, 2008
Sports Illustrated, Nov. 21, 2005, p.76; Feb. 12, 2007, p.32; Apr. 12, 2007, p.54; Apr. 17, 2008, p.50
Sports Illustrated for Kids, Mar. 1, 2006, p.44; July 2008, p.28
Time, Oct. 24, 2005, p.89
USA Today, Nov. 17, 2005, p.C1; Mar. 16, 2007, p.C1; Apr. 9, 2008, p.C11; June 20, 2008, p.C9

Online Articles

http://sports.espn.go.com
(ESPN, "Parker: First-Rate Game and a First-Rate Life," Dec. 4, 2007)
http://awards.honda.com
(Honda, "Collegiate Woman Athlete of the Year: Candace Parker," 2008)
http://www.nytimes.com
(New York Times, "Candace Parker Is Balancing Career and Family," Jan. 24, 2009)
http://sportsillustrated.cnn.com
(Sports Illustrated, "Parker Finding Balance between Motherhood, Basketball," July 6, 2009)
http://www.wnba.com
(WNBA, "Candace Parker Dishes on Her Award Haul, Her Winter Plans, and Her Father's Motivation," Oct. 4, 2008)

ADDRESS

Candace Parker
Los Angeles Sparks
888 South Figueroa Street, Ste. 2010
Los Angeles, CA 90017

WORLD WIDE WEB SITES

http://www.wnba.com/sparks
http://www.utladyvols.com

Kristen Stewart 1990-

American Actress

Plays Bella Swan in the *Twilight* Movie Series

BIRTH

Kristen Jaymes Stewart was born on April 9, 1990, in Los Angeles, California. Her mother, Jules, is Australian; she worked as a scriptwriter and script supervisor for movies and television shows. Her father, John, worked as a stage manager, producer, and director of television shows on the Fox network. Stewart has three older brothers.

YOUTH

Stewart grew up in Los Angeles. On vacations, her family often traveled to Australia to visit her mother's relatives and friends. That's where she discovered her love of surfing, a hobby she took up at an early age. She first learned to surf in Noosa Heads, a resort town in Queensland on the eastern coast of Australia. Noosa Heads is famous for its surfing beaches, which are common stops on the world competitive surfing circuit.

As a child, Stewart was not particularly interested in acting. Both of her parents and all of her brothers worked in the movie and television entertainment industry, but they all held jobs behind the camera. Stewart thought she might become a writer or director and never considered becoming an actor. "I never wanted to be the center of attention—I wasn't that 'I want to be famous, I want to be an actor' kid. I never sought out acting, but I always practiced my autograph because I loved pens. I'd write my name on everything."

BECOMING AN ACTRESS

Stewart started to change her mind about acting after taking part in her elementary school's holiday play one year. A talent agent happened to be in the audience, and her performance caught his attention. The next day, the agent called Stewart's parents to ask if she was interested in auditioning for acting roles. At first, her parents didn't like the idea. They were familiar with the movie and television industry and knew the challenges that child actors could face. Stewart was not sure about acting either, even though being in the school play had helped her realize that she liked performing on stage. After a lot of thought and discussion, she and her parents decided that she should try some auditions and see what happened. Stewart began auditioning for roles in movies and television shows when she was eight years old.

"I never wanted to be the center of attention—I wasn't that 'I want to be famous, I want to be an actor' kid. I never sought out acting, but I always practiced my autograph because I loved pens. I'd write my name on everything."

When she was 10 years old, Stewart got her first acting role after more than a year of going to auditions. She was given a small non-speaking part in the Disney Channel movie *The Thirteenth Year,* about a boy who discovers that his birth mother is a mermaid. This early experience helped convince her to continue her pursuit of an acting career.

Stewart appeared with Jody Foster in the 2002 thriller Panic Room.

CAREER HIGHLIGHTS

Almost from the beginning of her career, Stewart chose to follow a different path than most child actors. Rather than pursuing parts in television comedies and children's movies, Stewart wanted to play unusual young characters in serious dramatic movies. Her first speaking part was a small role in *The Safety of Objects,* an independent film released in 2001. The movie told the story of the overlapping lives of four families living in the same neighborhood, each struggling to cope with their own emotional problems. Stewart played Sam Jennings, the tomboy daughter of a troubled single mother. Although the movie was not received well by critics or moviegoers, the experience helped Stewart in future auditions.

The First Big Break

Stewart landed her first big role with a leading part in the 2002 psychological thriller *Panic Room.* This film told the suspenseful story of a single mother and her daughter who become trapped when a group of thieves break into their home. Stewart auditioned for the role of Sarah Altman, the young daughter of the character played by Jodie Foster. The audition process was long and difficult, including six different tryouts. Stewart was disappointed when the part was given to a different actress. However, a conflict in scheduling forced the original actress to back out of the project, and Stewart was offered the role after all.

Critics were unenthusiastic about *Panic Room* as a whole, but Stewart was praised for her believable performance. Many commented that she and Foster resembled each other so much and related so well to each other in the movie that they appeared to actually be mother and daughter. One writer for *Variety* said that Stewart "delivered an assured performance that led some critics to compare her skills to Foster's early style." A critic for *Interview* liked the "toughness and maturity" of her acting. Stewart was nominated for a Young Artist Award for her role in *Panic Room*.

"

"What I love about the [Twilight] *story is that it's about a very logical, pragmatic girl who you think would never get swept into something that has this bizarre power," Stewart said. "It's not an easy love. That's what I like about it. It's the most strained, impossible love, and they are both willing to fight for it and die for it. That's what I was drawn to."*

"

Stewart's successful performance in *Panic Room* led to her being cast in the 2003 film *Cold Creek Manor*. She played Kristen Tilson, the daughter of a couple who move their family into a house that they soon find seems to be haunted. This suspense drama did poorly with moviegoers and critics, although her performance earned her another Young Artist Award nomination.

Around this time, Stewart began homeschooling. Between going to auditions and acting in movies, it had become too difficult for her to conform to a traditional school schedule. Stewart missed a lot of school days when she was working on movies, and her grades began to suffer. "I started homeschooling because my teachers were failing me. I think it was just resentment—I made more work for them. But homeschooling is great; you can study what you want, which allows you to get more excited about what you're doing."

Soon after *Cold Creek Manor*, Stewart landed her first starring role in the 2004 movie *Catch That Kid*. She played the part of Maddy Phillips, a scheming 12-year-old super-spy. Maddy concocts an elaborate bank-robbing plan to get enough money to pay for the life-saving surgery needed by her dying father. This role allowed Stewart to show a different, lighter side of her acting ability. The movie also provided an opportunity for her to reach a younger audience, and it became a major hit with pre-teens. *Variety* called it a "breezy, teen-friendly caper," while a critic for the *Washington Post* said that her acting "perfectly captures the anxieties and frustrations of even the bravest pre-teen girl."

Stewart in a scene from Zathura, *based on the book by Chris Van Allsburg.*

The Fast Track to Stardom

Stewart was beginning to make a name for herself as a talented and versatile young actress who could hold her own playing dramatic roles opposite adult actors with much more experience. She was offered many more roles, and she appeared in 10 films made from 2005 to 2008. Stewart soon found herself on her way to becoming a movie star.

Stewart's next big project was the 2005 Showtime television movie *Speak,* based on the popular novel by Laurie Halse Anderson. Stewart played the starring role of Melinda Sordino, a high school freshman who stops almost all verbal communication after being raped by an upperclassman. This role provided her with the opportunity to portray different aspects of the same character, as Melinda struggles to put her life back together. Her performance was praised by critics, who called Stewart "breathtaking" and "a wonderfully expressive actress." A critic for the *New York Times* said that her performance "creates a convincing character full of pain and turmoil."

Also in 2005, Stewart appeared in *Zathura,* based on the book of the same name by Chris Van Allsburg. She played the older sister of two boys who find that playing a mysterious board game has accidentally transported the family home to the far reaches of outer space. This role allowed her to showcase her comic acting skills. Then in 2006, she had a leading role in *Fierce People,* the strange and dramatic story of a group of people brought together for a summer at the country estate of an aging billionaire. Neither of these movies enjoyed much commercial success, but Stewart continued to be noticed for her growing talent as an actress. By this time, she was moving from one project to the next almost continuously.

Stewart appeared in three movies released in 2007. She had a starring role as Jess Solomon in *The Messengers,* a moderately successful supernatural thriller about a family that moves from the city to an old farm. The farm quickly becomes the focus of many strange and unexplained events. Stewart followed this with a starring role as Lucy Hardwicke in the comedy/drama *In the Land of Women.* This movie tells the story of a young man who is transformed by his encounters with the family of women who live across the street from his grandmother. *Variety* called her performance the high point of the movie. *Variety* also praised her bold performance in *Into the Wild,* the story of a young man who leaves everything behind to travel through the Alaskan wilderness. Stewart was nominated for a Young Artist Award for her portrayal of Tracy Tatro, a teenager who falls in love with the idealistic young drifter.

— " —

"[Acting] just feels good. I find I want to do a movie because I love the script or I love the story. You have these themes in your mind, and you think about them incessantly, and then it's time to shoot the scene and you're like, 'Okay, you're going to be done with this in 15 minutes, so you'd better do it right.'"

— " —

Stewart continued her full work schedule, appearing in four movies released in 2008. In the Hollywood satire *What Just Happened?,* she played the rebellious daughter of an overwhelmed studio executive. Critics praised her performance as one of the most memorable parts of the film. In *The Yellow Handkerchief,* she starred as Martine, a young woman on a road trip through Louisiana who helps a hitchhiker who has just been released from prison to reunite with his wife. Stewart also had a very small part in *Jumper,* the story of a young man who is able to teleport to any location in the world. She appeared in the movie's final scene. But it was her fourth movie of 2008, *Twilight,* that would catapult her to superstardom.

Twilight

Twilight is the film adaptation of the popular young adult book of the same name by author Stephenie Meyer, the first book in a series of novels filled with romance, danger, and suspense. Stewart stars as Bella Swan, a teenager who moves to a rural small town in Washington state and soon becomes fascinated with the mysterious and handsome Edward Cullen (played by Robert Pattinson). Edward seems equally fascinated by Bella, and trouble brews for the two teens. Bella discovers that Edward is not really a teenager at all, but is in fact a very old vampire. And Edward struggles with his nearly overwhelming feelings for Bella, knowing how dangerous it is for him to even be near her. As Bella and Edward realize they are falling in love, danger gathers around them, until Bella must make a choice that deeply affects them both.

Before she auditioned for the role of Bella, Stewart had not read the *Twilight* books. When she read the film script, she was attacted to the idea of portraying a teenage girl who is experiencing such intense feelings of attraction for the first time. "What I love about the story is that it's about a very logical, pragmatic girl who you think would never get swept into something that has this bizarre power," Stewart said. "It's not an easy love. That's what I like about it. It's the most strained, impossible love, and they are both willing to fight for it and die for it. That's what I was drawn to." Before filming began, Stewart read the *Twilight* books to get a deeper sense of the character she was to play.

Filming *Twilight* proved somewhat challenging because for the first half of the production, Stewart was only 17 years old. As a minor, she was restricted by laws governing underage actors, so she could only work a maximum of five hours per day. Because her character Bella is in almost every scene of the movie, this made the shooting schedule difficult to manage. When Stewart had her 18th birthday in the middle of the production, *Twilight*'s director presented her with a cake decorated with a clock and the words "Now you're on nights," meaning that from that point on, Stewart had to work full days.

One of the most highly anticipated movies of 2008, *Twilight* earned mixed reviews from movie critics. *USA Today* offered some harsh comments. "Despite questionable casting, wooden acting, laughable dialogue, and truly awful makeup, nothing is likely to stop young girls from swarming to this kitschy adaptation of Stephenie Meyer's popular novel.... Stewart and Pat-

Stewart (Bella) with Robert Pattinson (Edward) and Taylor Lautner (Jacob) in scenes from Twilight *and* New Moon.

tinson lack chemistry. Her subtle acting does not serve her well in this overheated setting. As Bella, she seems to have two expressions: blank and slightly less blank." A reviewer for *Variety* called the movie "a disappointingly anemic tale of forbidden love that should satiate the pre-converted but will bewilder and underwhelm viewers who haven't devoured Stephenie Meyer's bestselling juvie chick-lit franchise.... A supernatural romance in which the supernatural and romantic elements feel rushed, unformed, and insufficiently motivated, leaving audiences with little to do but shrug and focus on the eye-candy." But the review went on to praise Stewart's performance, saying "Stewart makes Bella earthy, appealing, and slightly withdrawn." The *Washington Post* also pointed to her performance. "*Twilight* works as both love story and vampire story, thanks mainly to the performances of its principals. Pattinson and Stewart want to convince you that their characters are an undead freak and the girl who, against all logic, loves him. Yet they do it not by selling you on what makes Edward and Bella so different, but by finding their flesh-and-blood humanity."

"I'm really proud of *Twilight*," Stewart declared. "I think it's a good movie. It was hard to do, and I think it turned out pretty good." Fans agreed, as the movie became an immediate blockbuster hit. Fans were particularly drawn to the relationship between Bella and Edward, and that interest was fueled by rumors that Stewart and Pattinson were romantically involved. There have been many reports in celebrity magazines that claim it's true, but neither Stewart nor Pattinson have been willing to confirm it. Before the movie was even released, appearances by the pair drew wild crowds, as when 6,500 fans crowded a room at the 2008 Comic Con in San Diego just to get a glimpse of the *Twilight* cast in person. "It feels so good to have something you love be received so hotly," Stewart said of *Twilight*'s runaway success. "But the physical manifestation of the success, from the screaming fans to the box office, is just crazy." Indeed, the film's take at the box office was more than impressive. It earned almost $193 million in the U.S. and $385 million worldwide, with an opening weekend take of almost $70 million.

Twilight also earned multiple awards, sweeping the 2009 Teen Choice Awards by winning 11 of the 12 categories in which it was nominated. These included Stewart's award for Choice Movie Actress: Drama and the Choice Movie Liplock award, which she shared with her costar, Robert Pattinson. *Twilight* also won five MTV Movie Awards, including Best Female Performance for Stewart's portrayal of Bella, and the Best Kiss award shared by Stewart and Pattinson. She is proud of all of the awards, but shy about being honored for kissing. "I need to get over it," she revealed, "but I'm so concerned with what I look like during kissing scenes."

The closeness and chemistry that Stewart and Pattinson have shown onscreen, as in this scene from New Moon, *have led many to conclude that they are dating in real life.*

The Twilight Saga: New Moon

In *The Twilight Saga: New Moon,* Bella delves deeper into the mysteries of the supernatural world. The movie continues the love story between Bella and Edward, with all the passion, drama, suspense, and action of the original film. It starts with Bella's 18th birthday party going terribly wrong—she gets a minor paper cut that leads to a violent attack by one of the vampires. Edward knows he has to leave her to protect her, so he and his family leave town—and leave Bella heartbroken, numb, and alone. For solace she turns to her old friend Jacob, a member of the mysterious Quileute Indian tribe, who has a supernatural secret of his own. Things begin to develop between Bella and Jacob, but she still pines for Edward. He appears to her only when she's in danger, so she begins throwing herself into ever-more dangerous situations in hopes of summoning him. But finally, Bella goes too far.

When *The Twilight Saga: New Moon* was released in late 2009, it drew a mixed response from critics. The *New York Times* called it "the juiceless, near bloodless sequel." *Salon* criticized its pacing, complaining that "The movie is essentially a string of brooding speeches, often delivered in the woods, with very little interesting connective tissue in between.'" The *Boston Globe* called it "an anemic comedown after the full-blooded swoon of last year's *Twilight*.... [In most] respects, the movie's a drag—paced like a dirge and cursed with dialogue and a goopy musical score ... that bring out the book's worst daytime soap tendencies. But what can you expect from an installment that keeps the central duo of human Bella and vampire Edward apart for an extended 500-page sulk?" Others, though, enjoyed the movie's melodramatic aspects. *Slate* magazine called it a "juicebomb," a term to describe guilty pleasures, movies the reviewer couldn't intellectually defend but still loved. "*The Twilight Saga: New Moon*, like its 2008 predecessor *Twilight*, is a classic juicebomb. Mopey, draggy, and absurdly self-important, the movie nonetheless twangs at some resonant affective chord. This viewer, at least, was catapulted back to that moment of adolescence when being mopey, draggy, and absurdly self-important felt like a passionate act of liberation. The *Twilight* movies are schlock, but they're elegantly appointed, luxuriously enjoyable schlock, and the world they take place in—the densely forested, perpetually overcast, vampire-and-werewolf-ridden town of Forks, Wash.—feels like a real, if fantastical, place."

———— " ————

"If there is anything you really want to do, you have to give it a shot," Stewart stressed. "Otherwise you're going to hold onto it forever and just regret it. You should have no regret."

———— " ————

But whatever critics had to say about the film as a whole, they routinely praised Stewart. "The performances are uniformly strong, especially by Stewart, who is turning into a fine young actress," wrote the *Washington Post*. "Despite melodrama that, at times, is enough to induce diabetes, there's enough wolf whistle in this sexy, scary romp to please anyone." And *Salon* wrote that "Stewart is much better than she needs to be for this material: Even in the most emotionally heightened scenes, she intuitively eases up on the clutch—miraculously, nothing she does feels overdone or overthought."

Despite reviewers' ambivalence about the film, fans were smitten, turning out in droves as soon as it opened. *New Moon* earned almost $143 million on its first weekend, making it the biggest opening of 2009 and the third biggest opening behind only *The Dark Knight* and *Spider-Man 3*. Only a few weeks after its opening, *New Moon* had already earned more than $230 million in the U.S. and $473 million worldwide, and it showed no signs of slowing down. Fan interest was fueled by the ongoing rumors that

Stewart and Pattinson were dating in real life. In the meantime, fans are eagerly awaiting the opening of the next film in the series, *The Twilight Saga: Eclipse,* which is planned for June 2010.

Taking Roles in Other Films

Between the *Twilight* movies, Stewart worked on several other films. In fact, the success of the first film transformed her career. For example, *The Cake Eaters,* a movie that Stewart had completed before *Twilight,* had never been released. After the phenomenal success of *Twilight,* that movie suddenly had a 2009 release date and a poster that featured Stewart prominently. "If it was not for *Twilight,* I'm not sure *The Cake Eaters,* a film I dearly love, would have seen the light of day," Stewart remarked. In *The Cake Eaters,* she played Georgia, a young woman suffering from a debilitating disease. A reviewer for the *New York Times* praised her "tough, strong performance," and *Variety* called her acting excellent. A movie critic for the *Buffalo News* said, "Stewart is a superb young actress, and this is probably the most impressive thing she has yet done on film."

Stewart had a leading role in the 2009 comedy *Adventureland,* a story that takes place in 1987 and focuses on the experiences of a group of young people working at an amusement park in Pittsburgh, Pennsylvania. Stewart plays Em Lewin, who she described as "fairly damaged. She has an odd number of hang-ups. It's too much for her. Any time you don't like yourself people won't treat you well." The movie was not very successful in theaters, and it drew mixed reviews from critics. A reviewer for *USA Today* described the movie as a "bittersweet, if uneven, coming-of-age comedy" and said that Stewart's acting was "sullen and low-key." But *Entertainment Weekly* said that Stewart had "a cutting sharpness that draws you right to her pale, severe beauty."

Stewart also has a starring role in *Welcome to the Rileys,* a complex drama in which she played a teenaged stripper and prostitute. The story focuses on the makeshift family that gradually forms when her character joins up with a married couple who are grieving the death of their own daughter. *Welcome to the Rileys* is scheduled for release in 2009. She has also completed filming of *The Runaways,* the biographical story of the 1970s all-girl rock band led by Joan Jett, played by Stewart. *The Runaways* is scheduled for release in 2010. And of course, *The Twilight Saga: Eclipse* will apprear in 2010 as well.

Though she may have been reluctant initially to become an actress, Stewart now enjoys the challenge of making movies. "With acting, every story is different, and you're constantly playing different people, so you're never sure if you'll be able to pull it off. At the end it can be like the greatest thing

Stewart with Jesse Eisenberg in a scene from Adventureland.

in the world, but you have to second-guess yourself a little." Stewart has also said "[Acting] just feels good. I find I want to do a movie because I love the script or I love the story. You have these themes in your mind, and you think about them incessantly, and then it's time to shoot the scene and you're like, 'Okay, you're going to be done with this in 15 minutes, so you'd better do it right.'"

Overall, Stewart has earned consistently high praise from movie critics. One *Variety* writer said that Stewart is "an exceptionally poised young film actress with a knack for challenging roles as troubled adolescents" and that she impresses "audiences and critics alike with her realistic performances and her choice of projects." A writer in *Interview* said that her acting always "comes off 100 percent natural."

Even with all of her success, Stewart still isn't sure that she wants to stick with acting forever. "I want to go to college for literature," she stated. "I want to be a writer. I mean, I love what I do, but it's not all I want to do—be a professional liar for the rest of my life." But Stewart is happy that she made that long-ago decision to go on her first audition. "If there is anything you really want to do, you have to give it a shot," she stressed. "Otherwise you're going to hold onto it forever and just regret it. You should have no regret."

HOME AND FAMILY

Stewart lives in Los Angeles with her parents, a cat, and a border collie named Oz. She says she has "no plans to move any time soon. I'm really tight with my family and besides, I think it would be a little weird to have a big, sprawling place all on my own."

HOBBIES AND OTHER INTERESTS

When she is not busy filming or preparing for a movie, Stewart enjoys playing guitar and reading. She says her books are among her most prized possessions. "If my house were burning down, I'd be running out with all of my books." She also likes Big Band music and has recently taken up swing dancing. Stewart has also been an avid surfer since childhood. She visits Australia as often as she can, both for surfing and to visit friends and family there. "I love Australia and we have a lot of great family and friends down there. I can't wait to get back."

SELECTED CREDITS

The Safety of Objects, 2001
Panic Room, 2002
Cold Creek Manor, 2003
Catch That Kid, 2004
Speak, 2005
Zathura, 2005
Fierce People, 2006
In the Land of Women, 2007
The Messengers, 2007
Into the Wild, 2007
The Yellow Handkerchief, 2008
What Just Happened?, 2008
Twilight, 2008
The Cake Eaters, 2009
Adventureland, 2009
The Twilight Saga: New Moon, 2009

HONORS AND AWARDS

MTV Movie Awards: 2009 (two awards), Best Female Performance and Best Kiss (with Robert Pattinson), for *Twilight*
Teen Choice Awards: 2009 (two awards), Choice Movie Actress: Drama and Choice Movie Liplock (with Robert Pattinson), for *Twilight*

FURTHER READING

Books

Hurley, Jo. *Kristen Stewart: Bella of the Ball*, 2009

Periodicals

Entertainment Weekly, Nov. 14, 2008, p.30; Apr. 10, 2009, p.36; May 29, 2009, p.26; Nov. 20, 2009, p.30
Girls' Life, Apr./May 2007, p.37
Interview, Mar. 2006, p.167; Jan. 2007, p.136; Nov. 2007, p.110
Newsweek, Mar. 30, 2009, p.60
People, June 15, 2009, p.68; Nov. 2009 (special *New Moon* edition)
USA Today, Apr. 1, 2008, p.D1; Apr. 3, 2009, p.D13
Vanity Fair, Apr. 2007, p.201

Online Articles

http://www.mtv.com
(MTV, "*Twilight* Star Kristen Stewart Talks *New Moon*, Future Sequels," Mar. 17, 2009)
http://topics.newsweek.com/entertainment/movies/2009/twilight.htm
(Newsweek, "*Twilight*," collected articles, multiple dates)
http://www.teenink.com/nonfiction/celebrity_interviews
(TeenInk, "Actor—Kristen Stewart," no date)
http://www.usatoday.com/life/movies/news/2009-03-31-kristen-stewart_N.htm
(USA Today, "Kristen Stewart: Some People Think They Know Her, But . . ." Apr. 2, 2009)
http://www.variety.com
(Variety, "Kristen Stewart: Biography," 2009)

ADDRESS

Kristen Stewart
Summit Entertainment
1630 Stewart Street, Suite 120
Santa Monica, CA 90404

WORLD WIDE WEB SITES

http://www.twilightthemovie.com
http://www.newmoonthemovie.com/worldoftwilight
http://www.stepheniemeyer.com/twilightseries.html

Photo and Illustration Credits

Front Cover Photos: Beyoncé: Lewis Whyld/PA Photos/Landov; Hillary Rodham Clinton: Official Portrait of Secretary of State Hillary Clinton. Courtesy, State Department; Neil Gaiman: Jeffrey Mayer/WireImage; Brad Paisley: Ed Rode/Courtesy 2009 CMT Music Awards.

Beyoncé/Photos: Photo by Music World Entertainment/Nickelodeon via Image.net (p. 9); CD cover: THE WRITING'S ON THE WALL © 1999 Columbia Records/Sony BMG Music Entertainment. All Rights Reserved. (p. 12); Rick Diamond/WireImage (p. 14, top); Movie still: GOLDMEMBER . Photo by Melinda Sue Gordon/SMPSP © 2002 New Line Productions, Inc. All Rights Reserved. (p. 14, middle); CD Cover: DANGEROUSLY IN LOVE © 2003 Legacy/Columbia/Sony BMG Music Entertainment. All Rights Reserved. (p. 14, bottom); Courtesy MTV Networks (p. 17); Movie still: DREAMGIRLS. David James © 2006 Dreamworks LLC & Paramount Pictures. All Rights Reserved. (p. 19); CD Cover: I AM...SASHA FIERCE © 2008 Sony BMG Music Entertainment. All Rights Reserved. (p. 22); NBC Photo/Virginia Sherwood (p. 24).

Hillary Rodham Clinton/Photos: Official Portrait of Secretary of State Hillary Clinton. Courtesy, State Department (p. 29); Courtesy of William J. Clinton Presidential Library (p. 32); Photo from Persistence of Spirit Collection donated by Arkansas Democrat. Courtesy, Arkansas History Commission. (p. 35); U.S. Department of Defense (p. 37); AP Photo/Doug Mills (p. 38); AP Photo/Gerald Herbert (p. 40); Chris Fitzgerald/CandidatePhotos via Newscom (p. 43); Official White House photo by Pete Souza (p. 44, top); U.S. State Department photo (p. 44, middle and bottom).

Eran Egozy and Alex Rigopulos/Photos: Courtesy, Reverb Communications (p. 49); Courtesy Reverb Communications (p. 51); DVD Cover: AMPLITUDE © 2003 Sony Computer Entertainment America Inc. Developed by Harmonix Music Systems. (p. 55); DVD Cover: GUITAR HERO Game engine code © 2005 Harmonix Music Systems Inc. Developed by Harmonix Music Systems. © 2005 RedOctane, Inc. All Rights Reserved. (p. 58); THE BEATLES: ROCK BAND screenshot © 2009 Harmonix Music Systems, Inc. All Rights Reserved. (p. 61, top); ROCK BAND 2 screenshot © 2008 Harmonix Music Systems, Inc. All Rights Reserved. (p. 61, middle); ROCK BAND screenshot © 2008 Harmonix Music Systems, Inc. All Rights Reserved. (p. 61, bottom).

Neil Gaiman/Photos: Mark Sullivan/WireImage (p. 65); Xinhua/Landov (p. 67); Book cover: THE SANDMAN (Volume One); PRELUDES & NOCTURNES by Neil Gaiman. Published by DC Comics. Cover and compilation © 1991, 1995 DC Comics. All Rights Reserved. Cover and publication design by Dave McKean. (p. 70); Book cover: THE DAY I SWAPPED MY DAD FOR TWO GOLDFISH (HarperCollins Children's Books). © 1997, 2004 by Neil Gaiman and Dave McKean. (p. 72); Movie still: CORALINE © LAIKA, Inc. All Rights Reserved. (p. 75, top); Book cover: CORALINE (HarperCollins Publishers). Text © 2002 Neil Gaiman. Illustrations © 2002 Dave McKean. Jacket art © Dave McKean. Jacket design by Hilary Zarycky. (p. 75, middle); Movie still: CORALINE © LAIKA, Inc. All Rights Reserved. (p. 75, bottom); Book cover: MIRRORMASK © 2005 The Jim Henson Company (HarperCollins Children's Books). Text © 2005 by Neil Gaiman and Dave McKean. All Rights Reserved. (p. 77, top); Movie still: MIRRORMASK © 2005 The Jim Henson Company, Inc. All Rights Reserved. (p. 77, middle); Book cover: MIRRORMASK: THE ILLUSTRATED FILM SCRIPT OF THE MOTION PICTURE FROM THE JIM HENSON COMPANY. Script, storyboards, and artwork © 2005 The Jim Henson Company (William Morrow/imprint, HarperCollins Publishers).Text © 2005 by Neil Gaiman and Dave McKean. All Rights Reserved. (p. 77, bottom); Book cover: THE GRAVEYARD BOOK (HarperCollins Children's Books) Text © 2008 by Neil Gaiman. Illustrations © 2008 by Dave McKean. (p. 80).

Hugh Jackman/Photos: Antonio Nava/Landov (p. 85); Movie: X-MEN ORIGINS: WOLVERINE. Photo by James Fisher. (p. 88); Zuma Photos/Newscom (p. 90); Movie still: X2: X-MEN UNITED. Kerry Hayes/SMPSP ™ © 2003 Twentieth Century Fox. X-Men character likenesses: ™ © 2003 Marvel Characters, Inc. All Rights Reserved. (p. 92); Movie still: X-MEN 3: THE LAST STAND. Kerry Hayes/SMPSP ™ © 2006 Twentieth Century Fox. X-Men character likenesses: ™ © 2006 Marvel Characters, Inc. All Rights Reserved. (p. 94); Movie still: X-MEN ORIGINS: WOLVERINE. Photo by James Fisher. (p. 96); Movie still: HAPPY FEET © 2006 Warner Bros. All Rights Reserved. (p. 98, top); Publicity still: FLUSHED AWAY © 2006 Dreamworks Animated (p. 98, middle); Movie still: FLUSHED AWAY © 2006 Dreamworks Animated (p. 98, bottom).

Christianne Meneses Jacobs/Photos: Photo by Marc Jacobs/Courtesy Christianne Meneses Jacobs (pp. 103 and 106); Photo by James Dyrek/Courtesy Christianne Meneses Jacobs (p. 109); Photo by Rodney Choice/Courtesy Christianne Meneses Jacobs (p. 112).

Alexander Ovechkin/Photos: Jim McIsaac/Getty Images (p. 115); AP Photo/Jacques Boissinot (p. 116); Mitchell Layton/Getty Images (p. 119); AP Photo/Tom Mihalek (p. 121); AP Photo/Pablo Martinez Monsivais (p. 124).

Brad Paisley/Photos: ABC/Katherine Bomboy (p. 127); CD Cover: WHO NEEDS PICTURES © 1999 Arista Records/BMG Entertainment. All Rights Reserved. (p. 130); AP Photo/The Tennessean/Randy Piland (p. 132); ABC/Katherine Bomboy (p. 134); CD Cover: AN AMERICAN SATURDAY NIGHT © 2009 Arista Nashville/ Sony BMG Music Entertainment. All Rights Reserved. (p. 137); Official White House photo by Pete Souza (p. 139).

Candace Parker/Photos: Greg Ashman/CSM/Landov (p. 143); Dwain Scott/WireImage (p. 145); Courtesy of Tennessee Athletics Media Relations (p. 147); AP Photo/Paul Connors (p. 151).

Kristen Stewart/Photos: Picture Group/MTV (p. 155); Movie still: PANIC ROOM © 2002 Columbia Pictures Industries, Inc. All Rights Reserved. (p. 157); Movie still:

Cumulative Names Index

This cumulative index includes the names of all individuals profiled in *Biography Today* since the debut of the series in 1992.

For cumulative general, places of birth, and birthday indexes, please see biographytoday.com.

For cumulative general, places of birth, and birthday indexes, please see biographytoday.com.

For cumulative general, places of birth, and birthday indexes, please see biographytoday.com.

For cumulative general, places of birth, and birthday indexes, please see biographytoday.com.